NEW YORK TEST PREP

Common Core

Mathematics

Practice Workbook

Grade 5

ISBN 978-1727364460

TEST MASTER PRESS

www.testmasterpress.com

CONTENTS

INTRODUCTION
For Parents, Teachers, and Tutors

About the New York Mathematics Tests

Students in New York will be assessed by taking the New York State Mathematics tests. This practice workbook will prepare students for the tests. It contains four warm-up practice sets that will introduce students to all the types of questions found on the test. This is followed by practice sets that mimic the content of the two test sessions on the real state tests.

Warm-Up Sets

The warm-up sets are short tests that will introduce students to the tests and give them practice before taking the full-length practice sets. They include the types of questions students will encounter on the real tests, with a strong focus on more rigorous short-response and extended-response questions. The first two tests contains 10 questions each and the second two tests contain 20 questions each.

Practice Sets

The mini-tests are followed by full-length practice sets that are similar to the test sessions that students complete on the real tests. On the real tests, Session 1 contains 30 multiple-choice questions. Session 2 contains 8 multiple-choice questions, 6 short-response questions, and 1 extended-response question. This practice book has practice sets of 30 multiple-choice questions and practice sets of 10 short-response and extended-response questions. The additional short-response and extended-response questions will ensure that all the skills are covered and will give students more practice applying skills and answering complex questions.

Calculators and Tools

Students should be provided with a ruler to use on all parts of the test. Students are not allowed to use a calculator on any part of the tests, and so should complete all the practice tests without the use of a calculator.

About the Next Generation Learning Standards

In 2017, the state of New York introduced the Next Generation Learning Standards. These are revised standards that replace the previous Common Core Learning Standards, though remain very close in content. State testing will continue to assess the Common Core Learning Standards until 2020, but the new standards will be gradually implemented over this time. This workbook has aligned all questions to the new Next Generation Learning Standards. However, the questions still also cover the Common Core standards that are assessed on the state tests.

Common Core Mathematics

Practice Set 1

Mixed Questions

Instructions

Read each question carefully. For each multiple-choice question, fill in the circle for the correct answer. For other types of questions, follow the directions given in the question.

You may use a ruler and a protractor to help you answer questions. You may not use a calculator on this test. You may also use the reference information below.

Conversions

1 mile = 5,280 feet	1 pound = 16 ounces	1 cup = 8 fluid ounces
1 mile = 1,760 yards	1 ton = 2,000 pounds	1 pint = 2 cups
		1 quart = 2 pints
		1 gallon = 4 quarts
		1 liter = 1,000 cubic centimeters

Formulas

Right Rectangular Prism $V = Bh$ or $V = lwh$

1   Tim plotted four points on the coordinate grid below. Which point would be 5 units from the origin and on the *x*-axis?

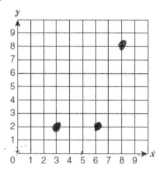

Ⓐ   (0, 0)

Ⓑ   (0, 5)

●   (5, 0)

Ⓓ   (5, 5)

2   The grid below represents the calculation of 0.4 × 0.2.

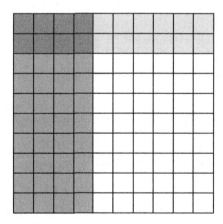

What is the value of 0.4 × 0.2? Write your answer below.

_____

3 Jonah filled the box below with 1-inch cubes. How many 1-inch cubes would it take to fill the box?

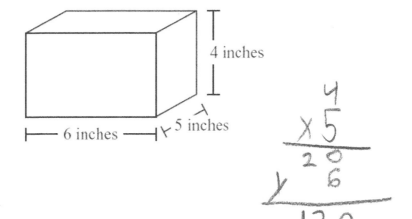

Ⓐ   15

Ⓑ   30

Ⓒ   60

Ⓓ   120

4 Which ordered pair represents a point located on the line?

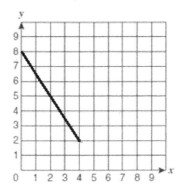

Ⓐ   (8, 0)

Ⓑ   (4, 2)

Ⓒ   (3, 3)

Ⓓ   (5, 2)

5   Place the sign <, >, or = in each empty box to correctly compare each pair of decimals.

0.06 $\boxed{>}$ 0.006

1.22 $\boxed{<}$ 1.42

5.669 $\boxed{>}$ 5.667

7.535 $\boxed{>}$ 7.505

0.85 $\boxed{=}$ 0.850

9.077 $\boxed{<}$ 9.770

6   Don spends $12.80 on four sandwiches. If each sandwich has the same cost, what is the cost of each sandwich?

Show your work.

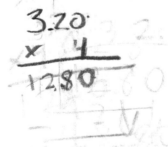

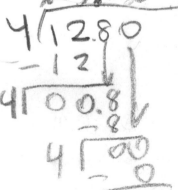

Answer _____

7   A pattern has the rule $y = x$. A second pattern has the rule $y = x + 2$.

Complete the tables below to find the value of y for each value of x for the

two patterns. Then plot both lines on the coordinate grid.

$y = x$

x	y
0	
1	
2	
3	

$y = x + 2$

x	y
0	
1	
2	
3	

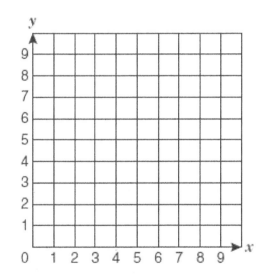

On the lines below, compare the lines on the coordinate grid.

_____

_____

_____

_____

8   Lisa filled the box below with 1-centimeter cubes.

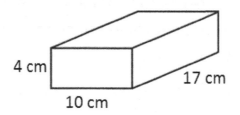

4 cm

17 cm

10 cm

How many 1-centimeter cubes would it take to fill the box?

Show your work.

Answer _____

9   Complete the missing numbers to write 300,000 in four more different ways.

30,000   tens

_____ hundreds

_____ thousands

_____ ten-thousands

_____ hundred-thousands

10   Place the shapes listed below in the correct section of the Venn diagram.

rhombus   rectangle   square

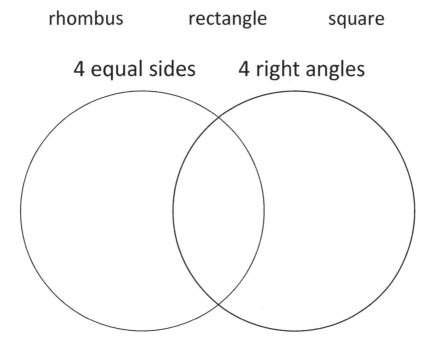

4 equal sides   4 right angles

END OF PRACTICE SET

Common Core Mathematics

Practice Set 2

Mixed Questions

Instructions

Read each question carefully. For each multiple-choice question, fill in the circle for the correct answer. For other types of questions, follow the directions given in the question.

You may use a ruler and a protractor to help you answer questions. You may not use a calculator on this test. You may also use the reference information below.

Conversions

1 mile = 5,280 feet	1 pound = 16 ounces	1 cup = 8 fluid ounces
1 mile = 1,760 yards	1 ton = 2,000 pounds	1 pint = 2 cups
		1 quart = 2 pints
		1 gallon = 4 quarts
		1 liter = 1,000 cubic centimeters

Formulas

Right Rectangular Prism $V = Bh$ or $V = lwh$

1   Jezebel plots the point (3, 5) on a coordinate grid. Which of these describes where the point would be plotted?

Ⓐ   3 units up from the origin and 5 units left of the *y*-axis

Ⓑ   3 units up from the origin and 5 units right of the *y*-axis

Ⓒ   3 units to the left of the origin and 5 units up from the *x*-axis

Ⓓ   3 units to the right of the origin and 5 units up from the *x*-axis

2   The table shows the best times for running 100 meters of four students on the track team.

Student	Best Time (seconds)
Ramon	12.77
Ellis	12.63
Xavier	12.75
Colin	12.68

If each time is rounded to the nearest tenth, which student would have a best time of 12.7 seconds?

Ⓐ   Ramon

Ⓑ   Ellis

Ⓒ   Xavier

Ⓓ   Colin

3   Annabelle has 56 1-centimeter cubes. What are the dimensions of a rectangular prism Annabelle could build with all the cubes?

Ⓐ   7 units long, 4 units high, 2 units wide

Ⓑ   6 units long, 5 units high, 5 units wide

Ⓒ   10 units long, 2 units high, 3 units wide

Ⓓ   8 units long, 2 units high, 4 units wide

4   Circle the calculation that is represented on the grid below. Then find the value of the calculation.

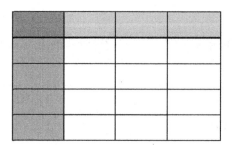

$0.25 \div 0.2$ $0.25 \div 4$ $0.2 \div 4$ $0.2 \div 5$

Answer _____

5   Select **all** the expressions below that are equal to $\frac{2}{3}$.

☐ $\frac{1}{3} \times \frac{1}{3}$

☐ $\frac{1}{6} + \frac{1}{6}$

☐ $\frac{1}{3} + \frac{1}{3}$

☐ $\frac{1}{6} \times \frac{1}{6}$

☐ $3 - \frac{1}{3}$

☐ $\frac{5}{12} + \frac{3}{12}$

6   Bryant was reading a book with 220 pages. He read 90 pages in the first week. He wants to finish the book in 5 days. Write an expression that can be used to calculate how many pages he needs to read each day to finish the book in 5 days. Then simplify the expression to find the number of pages he needs to read each day.

Expression _____

Answer _____

7   A factory can fill 225 bottles of orange juice each hour. Each bottle of juice contains 24 fluid ounces of juice. Each bottle of juice sells for $5.50.

How many bottles of juice can be filled in each 12-hour shift? Write your answer below.

_____

If all the bottles made in a 12-hour shift sell, how much money will be made? Write your answer below.

_____

How many fluid ounces of juice are filled in each 12-hour shift? Write your answer below.

_____ fluid ounces

How many pints of juice are filled in each 12-hour shift? Write your answer below.

_____ pints

8   During a science experiment, Holly measured the lengths of ten acorns she collected. The lengths, in inches, are listed below.

$$1\frac{1}{4}, \; 1\frac{5}{8}, \; 1\frac{1}{2}, \; 1\frac{1}{2}, \; 1\frac{1}{4}, \; 1\frac{1}{8}, \; 1\frac{1}{4}, \; 1\frac{1}{2}, \; 1\frac{1}{4}, \; 1\frac{3}{8}$$

Use the data to complete the line plot below.

Acorns

$$1\frac{1}{8} \qquad 1\frac{1}{4} \qquad 1\frac{3}{8} \qquad 1\frac{1}{2} \qquad 1\frac{5}{8}$$

Length (inches)

What is the difference between the longest and the shortest acorn? Write your answer below.

_____ inches

9   A pattern has the rule $y = 2x + 2$. Complete the table below to find the value of y for each value of x.

x	y
0	
1	
2	
3	

Plot the points from the table on the coordinate grid below and draw the line that connects the points.

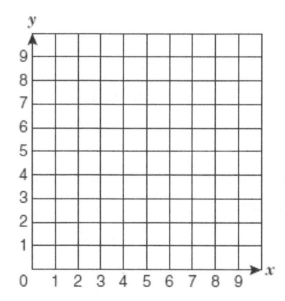

10 Write the names of the shapes below in the correct section of the Venn diagram.

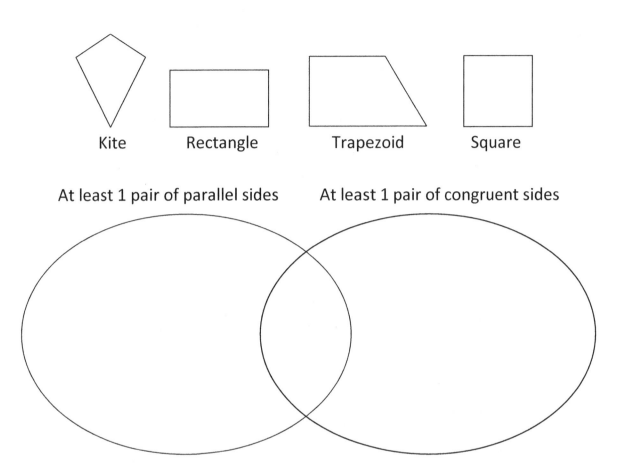

END OF PRACTICE SET

Common Core Mathematics

Practice Set 3

Mixed Questions

Instructions

Read each question carefully. For each multiple-choice question, fill in the circle for the correct answer. For other types of questions, follow the directions given in the question.

You may use a ruler and a protractor to help you answer questions. You may not use a calculator on this test. You may also use the reference information below.

Conversions

1 mile = 5,280 feet	1 pound = 16 ounces	1 cup = 8 fluid ounces
1 mile = 1,760 yards	1 ton = 2,000 pounds	1 pint = 2 cups
		1 quart = 2 pints
		1 gallon = 4 quarts
		1 liter = 1,000 cubic centimeters

Formulas

Right Rectangular Prism $V = Bh$ or $V = lwh$

1   The table below shows the ticket prices for a bus tour.

Ticket	Price
Adult	$5
Child	$3
Senior	$4

Sam's family paid exactly $15 for bus tickets. Which set of tickets could they have bought?

Ⓐ   1 adult, 2 child, and 1 senior

Ⓑ   2 adult, 1 child

Ⓒ   1 adult, 1 child, 2 senior

Ⓓ   3 child, 1 senior

2   Amanda plotted the four points below on a coordinate grid.

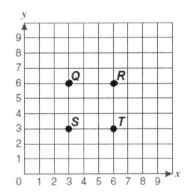

Amanda plots a fifth point that is an equal distance from two of the points. Which of these could be the coordinates of the fifth point?

Ⓐ   (5, 8)

Ⓑ   (3.5, 5)

Ⓒ   (7, 7)

Ⓓ   (9, 4.5)

3   A bakery sold 0.25 of its apple pies by lunch time. What fraction of the apple pies were sold by lunch time?

Ⓐ $\dfrac{1}{25}$

Ⓑ $\dfrac{1}{4}$

Ⓒ $\dfrac{2}{5}$

Ⓓ $\dfrac{3}{4}$

4   Look at the Venn diagram below. Which shape should be placed in the overlapping section of the diagram?

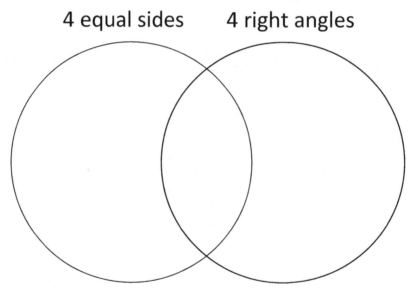

Ⓐ   Rectangle

Ⓑ   Rhombus

Ⓒ   Trapezoid

Ⓓ   Square

5 Jed has 12 dimes, 18 nickels, and 42 pennies. What is the greatest common factor Jed can use to divide the coins into equal piles?

Ⓐ   2

Ⓑ   4

Ⓒ   6

Ⓓ   12

6 Erin is sorting 65 quarters into piles. She puts the quarters in piles of 5.

How many piles of dimes would Erin have?

Ⓐ   11

Ⓑ   13

Ⓒ   15

Ⓓ   17

7   Joanne had three singing lessons one week. Two lessons went for 45 minutes, and one lesson went for 60 minutes. Which number sentence could be used to find how many minutes Joanne had singing lessons for?

Ⓐ   (2 x 45) x 60

Ⓑ   (2 + 45) x 60

Ⓒ   (2 x 45) + 60

Ⓓ   (2 + 45) + 60

8   A school has 7 school buses. Each bus can seat 48 students. A total of 303 students get on the buses to go to a school camp. How many empty seats would there be on the buses?

Show your work.

Answer _____

9   What is the value of the expression below?

$$(16 + 20) - 8 \div 4$$

Show your work.

Answer _____

10   A jug of milk contains 3 quarts of milk. Michael pours 1 pint of milk from the jug. How many pints of milk are left in the jug?

Show your work.

Answer _____ pints

11   A talent contest will go for 100 minutes. The contest is divided into 16 equal segments. How long will each segment go for? Write your answer below as a fraction in lowest form.

You can use the hundreds grid below to help you find your answer.

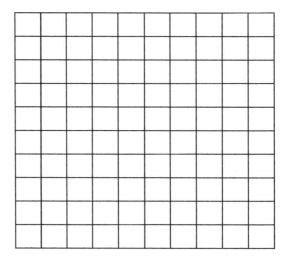

_____ minutes

12   Mike went on vacation to Ohio. When he left home, the odometer read 7,219.4 miles. When he returned home, the odometer read 8,192.6 miles. How many miles did Mike travel?

Show your work.

Answer _____ miles

13   The table below shows the prices of items at a cake stall.

Item	Price
Small cake	$1.85
Muffin	$2.25
Cookie	$0.95

Frankie bought a small cake and a cookie. Bronwyn bought a muffin. How much more did Frankie spend than Bronwyn?

Show your work.

Answer _____

14   The grid below represents Dani's living room.

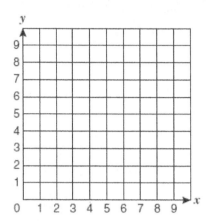

The television is located at the point (5, 4). A lamp is sitting 4 units to the right of the television and 3 units down from the television. What ordered pair represents the location of the lamp?

Answer _____

Explain how you found your answer.

_____

_____

_____

_____

15   Justine drew the triangle XYZ below.

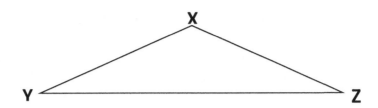

Based on the side lengths, what type of triangle is XYZ? Write your answer below.

_____

Explain why you classified the triangle that way.

_____

_____

_____

_____

_____

16   The table shows the cost of hiring DVDs for different numbers of DVDs.

Number of DVDs (d)	Total Cost, in Dollars (C)
2	6
5	15
6	18
8	24

Which equation shows the relationship between the number of DVDs hired, *d*, and the total cost in dollars, *C*?

Ⓐ $C = d + 4$

Ⓑ $C = 2d + 2$

Ⓒ $C = 3d$

Ⓓ $C = d + 10$

17   Which of the following shapes is a pentagon?

Ⓐ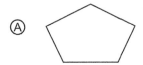

Ⓑ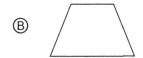

Ⓒ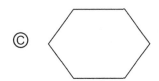

Ⓓ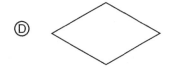

18 At the start of the week, a plant had a height of $\frac{5}{8}$ inches. The plant grew $\frac{1}{4}$ of an inch during the week. Which diagram is shaded to show the height of the plant at the end of the week?

Ⓐ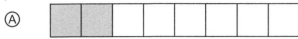

Ⓑ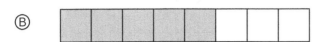

Ⓒ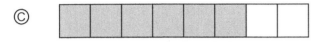

Ⓓ

19 On May 1, Felipe paid $3.58 per gallon of fuel. On August 1, Felipe paid $3.71 per gallon of fuel. By how much did the price of fuel increase?

Ⓐ $0.03

Ⓑ $0.07

Ⓒ $0.13

Ⓓ $0.17

20 Which operation in the expression should be carried out first?

$$6 + 3 \times (8 - 2 \times 2)$$

Ⓐ $6 + 3$

Ⓑ 3×8

Ⓒ $8 - 2$

Ⓓ 2×2

END OF PRACTICE SET

Common Core Mathematics

Practice Set 4

Mixed Questions

Instructions

Read each question carefully. For each multiple-choice question, fill in the circle for the correct answer. For other types of questions, follow the directions given in the question.

You may use a ruler and a protractor to help you answer questions. You may not use a calculator on this test. You may also use the reference information below.

Conversions

1 mile = 5,280 feet	1 pound = 16 ounces	1 cup = 8 fluid ounces
1 mile = 1,760 yards	1 ton = 2,000 pounds	1 pint = 2 cups
		1 quart = 2 pints
		1 gallon = 4 quarts
		1 liter = 1,000 cubic centimeters

Formulas

Right Rectangular Prism $V = Bh$ or $V = lwh$

1   Shade the diagrams below to show the subtraction. Then write the correct
     answer below on the blank line.

$$\frac{5}{8} \quad - \quad \frac{1}{4} \quad = \quad \underline{\hspace{2cm}}$$

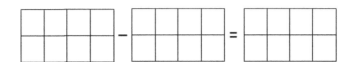

2   Kayla studied for a total of 150 minutes. She spent 50 minutes studying
     Spanish. What fraction of her total study time did she spend studying
     Spanish?

     Ⓐ $\frac{1}{5}$

     Ⓑ $\frac{1}{4}$

     Ⓒ $\frac{1}{3}$

     Ⓓ $\frac{1}{2}$

3   An orange tree has a height of 2.45 meters. What is the height of the tree in centimeters?

   Ⓐ   24.5 cm

   Ⓑ   245 cm

   Ⓒ   2,450 cm

   Ⓓ   24,500 cm

4   Which diagram represents the sum of $\frac{1}{4}$ and $\frac{1}{8}$?

   Ⓐ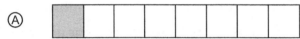

   Ⓑ

   Ⓒ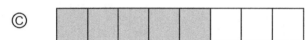

   Ⓓ

5   Which number is less than 35.052?

   Ⓐ   35.009

   Ⓑ   35.061

   Ⓒ   35.101

   Ⓓ   35.077

6   The table below shows a set of number pairs.

x	y
1	2
3	5
5	9

If the points were plotted on a coordinate grid, which of the following would be the coordinates of one of the points?

Ⓐ   (0, 0)

Ⓑ   (2, 1)

Ⓒ   (3, 5)

Ⓓ   (4, 6)

7   A pattern of numbers is shown below.

8, 13, 18, 23, 28, 33, 38, …

Which number would be a number in the pattern?

Ⓐ   41

Ⓑ   53

Ⓒ   65

Ⓓ   76

8   An orchard has a total of 192 orange trees. They are planted in rows of 12 orange trees each. How many rows of orange trees does the orchard have?

Show your work.

Answer _____

9   Joshua bought a pair of sunglasses for $14.85 and a phone case for $2.55. How much change should he receive from $20?

Show your work.

Answer _____

10   The model below was made with 1-inch cubes.

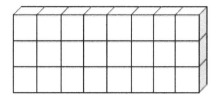

What is the volume of the model? Be sure to include the correct units in your answer.

Show your work.

Answer _____

11   The graph below shows a line segment with 3 points marked.

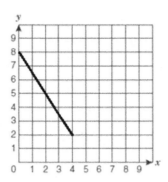

Part A

Complete the table below to show the coordinates of 3 points the line passes through.

x	0	2	4
y			

Part B

What are the coordinates of the point where the line intercepts the *y*-axis?

Answer _____

12 Candice has a painting canvas that is $\frac{3}{4}$ foot long and $\frac{3}{4}$ foot wide. What is the area of the canvas? Shade the diagram below to find the area of the canvas. Write your answer below.

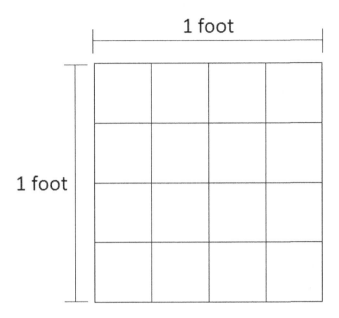

Area _____ square feet

13   Jasper made a flag for his football team. He painted $\frac{1}{2}$ of the flag blue and $\frac{1}{2}$ of the flag yellow. He added stars to $\frac{1}{3}$ of the blue section. What fraction of the total flag is the blue section with stars?

Show your work.

Answer _____

14   Shade the model below to show $1\frac{2}{5}$.

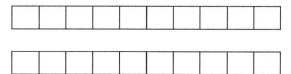

Use the model to find the value of $1\frac{2}{5} \div 2$. Write your answer below.

_____

On the lines below, explain how you found your answer.

_____

_____

_____

_____

_____

15   What are the two smallest 3-digit numbers that can be made using the digits 5, 7, and 2? Each digit must be used only once in each number. Write the two numbers below.

_____ and _____

On the lines below, explain how you found your answer.

_____

_____

_____

_____

_____

16   How is the numeral 55.12 written in words?

Ⓐ   Fifty-five hundred and twelve

Ⓑ   Fifty-five and twelve thousandths

Ⓒ   Fifty-five and twelve hundredths

Ⓓ   Fifty-five and twelve

17 It took James and his family $2\frac{1}{4}$ hours to drive from their house to the beach. How many minutes did the drive take?

Ⓐ   75 minutes

Ⓑ   135 minutes

Ⓒ   145 minutes

Ⓓ   225 minutes

18 A cat weighs 9 pounds. How many ounces does the cat weigh?

Ⓐ   36 oz

Ⓑ   108 oz

Ⓒ   144 oz

Ⓓ   72 oz

19 What is the value of 10^3?

Ⓐ   30

Ⓑ   100

Ⓒ   1,000

Ⓓ   3,000

20   Which pairs of numbers could be added to the table below?

Number	Number ÷ 10
85.04	8.504
501.62	50.162
19.483	1.9483

Ⓐ

28.63	286.3

Ⓑ

62.69	0.6269

Ⓒ

7.25	72.5

Ⓓ

46.77	4.677

END OF PRACTICE SET

Common Core Mathematics

Practice Set 5

Multiple-Choice Questions

Instructions

Read each question carefully. For each multiple-choice question, fill in the circle for the correct answer.

You may use a ruler and a protractor to help you answer questions. You may not use a calculator on this test. You may also use the reference information below.

Conversions

1 mile = 5,280 feet	1 pound = 16 ounces	1 cup = 8 fluid ounces
1 mile = 1,760 yards	1 ton = 2,000 pounds	1 pint = 2 cups
		1 quart = 2 pints
		1 gallon = 4 quarts
		1 liter = 1,000 cubic centimeters

Formulas

Right Rectangular Prism $V = Bh$ or $V = lwh$

1   To add the fractions below, Wayne first needs to determine the least common multiple of the denominators.

$$\frac{1}{5}, \frac{5}{7}, \frac{9}{10}$$

What is the least common multiple of the denominators?

Ⓐ   35

Ⓑ   50

Ⓒ   70

Ⓓ   350

2   The diagram below shows the length of a piece of ribbon.

$$\frac{12}{100} \text{ meter}$$

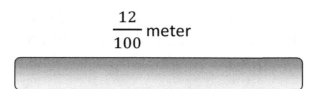

Victoria divides the lace into 4 equal pieces. What is the length of each piece of lace?

Ⓐ $\frac{2}{25}$ meter

Ⓑ $\frac{3}{25}$ meter

Ⓒ $\frac{12}{25}$ meter

Ⓓ $\frac{3}{100}$ meter

3   Donna has $8.45. She spends $3.75. How much money does Donna have left?

    Ⓐ $3.70

    Ⓑ $3.30

    Ⓒ $4.70

    Ⓓ $4.30

4   Hannah cut out a piece of fabric to use for an art project. The length of the fabric was 9.5 yards. The width of the fabric was 3.6 yards less than the length. What was the width of the fabric?

    Ⓐ   5.9 yards

    Ⓑ   6.9 yards

    Ⓒ   12.1 yards

    Ⓓ   13.1 yards

5   Errol is putting photos into albums. Each album has 24 pages for holding photos, and each page can hold 8 photographs. How many photographs could Errol put into 3 photo albums?

    Ⓐ   192

    Ⓑ   376

    Ⓒ   486

    Ⓓ   576

6   Kathy answered $\frac{3}{5}$ of the questions on a test correctly. Which of the

following is equivalent to $\frac{3}{5}$?

Ⓐ   0.3

Ⓑ   0.35

Ⓒ   0.6

Ⓓ   0.65

7   Which ordered pair represents a point where the edges of the two rectangles intersect?

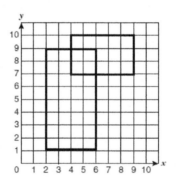

Ⓐ   (8, 6)

Ⓑ   (6, 7)

Ⓒ   (5, 8)

Ⓓ   (4, 10)

8 To complete a calculation correctly, Mark moves the decimal place of 420.598 two places to the left.

$$420.598 \rightarrow 4.20598$$

Which of these describes the calculation completed?

 Ⓐ Dividing by 10

 Ⓑ Dividing by 100

 Ⓒ Multiplying by 10

 Ⓓ Multiplying by 100

9 Camille cooked a cake on high for $1\frac{1}{4}$ hours. She then cooked it for another $\frac{1}{2}$ hour on low. How long did she cook the cake for in all?

 Ⓐ $1\frac{1}{2}$ hours

 Ⓑ $1\frac{3}{4}$ hours

 Ⓒ $2\frac{1}{4}$ hours

 Ⓓ $2\frac{1}{2}$ hours

10   A play sold $222 worth of tickets. Each ticket cost the same amount. Which of these could be the cost of each ticket?

Ⓐ $6

Ⓑ $8

Ⓒ $12

Ⓓ $16

11   A piece of note paper has side lengths of 12.5 centimeters. What is the area of the piece of note paper?

Ⓐ   144.25 square centimeters

Ⓑ   144.5 square centimeters

Ⓒ   156.25 square centimeters

Ⓓ   156.5 square centimeters

12   Cody drew a quadrilateral on a coordinate grid, as shown below.

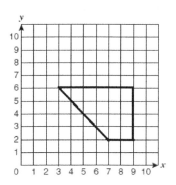

Which of these is NOT the coordinates of one of the vertices of the quadrilateral?

Ⓐ   (7, 2)

Ⓑ   (9, 2)

Ⓒ   (6, 9)

Ⓓ   (3, 6)

13   Sandy has $12.90. Marvin has $18.50. What is the total value of their money?

Ⓐ $20.40

Ⓑ $21.40

Ⓒ $30.40

Ⓓ $31.40

14 The top of a desk is 4 feet long and 3 feet wide. Raymond wants to cover the top of the desk with a vinyl sheet. The vinyl sheet is measured in square inches. What is the area of the vinyl sheet that will cover the top of the desk exactly?

    Ⓐ   12 square inches

    Ⓑ   144 square inches

    Ⓒ   168 square inches

    Ⓓ   1,728 square inches

15 A block is in the shape of a cube. If the side length is represented by x, which of these could be used to find the volume of the cube?

    Ⓐ $3x$

    Ⓑ $6(x^2)$

    Ⓒ $6x$

    Ⓓ x^3

16　Denise made the line plot below to show how long she read for each weekday for 4 weeks.

Daily Reading Time (hours)

```
                                    X
        X                           X
        X                 X         X
        X                 X         X         X
        X         X       X         X         X
        X         X       X         X         X
    ─────────────────────────────────────────────
        0         1       1         3         1
                  ─       ─         ─
                  4       2         4
```

How long did Denise read for in total over the 4 weeks?

Ⓐ　8 hours

Ⓑ　9 hours

Ⓒ　10 hours

Ⓓ　11 hours

17   The point below is translated 2 units to the left and 3 units down. What are the coordinates of the point after the translation?

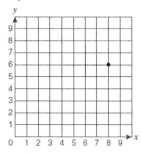

Ⓐ   (6, 3)

Ⓑ   (6, 9)

Ⓒ   (10, 3)

Ⓓ   (10, 9)

18   The table below shows the total number of pounds of flour in different numbers of bags of flour.

Number of Bags	Number of Pounds
3	12
5	20
8	32
9	36

Based on the relationship in the table, how many ounces of flour are in each bag?

Ⓐ   4 ounces

Ⓑ   12 ounces

Ⓒ   64 ounces

Ⓓ   192 ounces

19   The model below is made up of 1-centimeter cubes. What is a correct way to find the volume of the model?

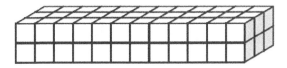

Ⓐ   12 cm x 6 cm

Ⓑ   12 cm x 12 cm

Ⓒ   2 cm x 6 cm x 12 cm

Ⓓ   2 cm x 3 cm x 12 cm

20   Which decimal is plotted on the number line below?

Ⓐ   2.25

Ⓑ   2.3

Ⓒ   2.6

Ⓓ   2.75

21   Brian made 16 paper cranes in 15 minutes. If he continues making cranes at this rate, how many cranes would he make in 2 hours?

Ⓐ   64

Ⓑ   120

Ⓒ   128

Ⓓ   480

22   The wingspan of the butterfly is 6.7 centimeters.

What is the wingspan of the butterfly in millimeters?

Ⓐ   0.067 mm

Ⓑ   0.67 mm

Ⓒ   67 mm

Ⓓ   670 mm

23   Jason used cubes to make the model shown below. What is the volume of the model?

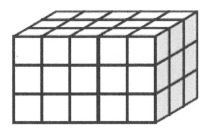

   Ⓐ   15 cubic units

   Ⓑ   45 cubic units

   Ⓒ   50 cubic units

   Ⓓ   75 cubic units

24   The pattern below starts at 0 and uses the rule "Add 4."

0, 4, 8, 12, 16

A second pattern starts at 2 and uses the rule "Add 4." How does the fifth term in the second pattern compare to the fifth term in the first pattern?

   Ⓐ   It is 2 greater.

   Ⓑ   It is 4 greater.

   Ⓒ   It is 8 greater.

   Ⓓ   It is 10 greater.

25   The table below shows a set of number pairs.

x	y
2	−2
3	0
4	2

If the points were plotted on a coordinate grid, which of the following would be the coordinates of one of the points?

Ⓐ   (0, 2)

Ⓑ   (2, 2)

Ⓒ   (4, 2)

Ⓓ   (3, 4)

26   The Greenway Softball Club made $2,160 by holding a talent night. The softball club wants to divide the money evenly between the 12 teams in the club. How much will each team receive?

Ⓐ $120

Ⓑ $140

Ⓒ $160

Ⓓ $180

27 The shaded parts of the model represent a fraction.

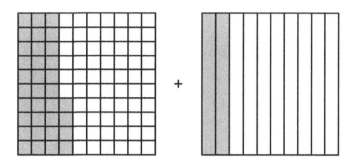

What is the sum of the fractions?

Ⓐ $\dfrac{36}{100}$

Ⓑ $\dfrac{54}{100}$

Ⓒ $\dfrac{36}{110}$

Ⓓ $\dfrac{54}{110}$

28 Winona has 48 stamps. She has 6 times as many stamps as Catherine. How many stamps does Catherine have?

Ⓐ 8

Ⓑ 9

Ⓒ 42

Ⓓ 288

29 The line plot below shows data a science class collected on the diameter of pebbles collected on a beach.

Pebble Diameter (inches)

```
              X
              X                   X       X
              X       X       X   X   X       X
    ─────────────────────────────────────────────
      0      1/8    1/4    3/8   1/2  5/8  3/4  7/8   1
```

How much greater was the diameter of the largest pebble than the smallest pebble?

Ⓐ $\frac{3}{4}$ inches

Ⓑ $\frac{3}{8}$ inches

Ⓒ $\frac{5}{8}$ inches

Ⓓ $\frac{7}{8}$ inches

30 What is the value of $\frac{9}{12} - \frac{3}{12}$?

Ⓐ $\frac{1}{12}$

Ⓑ $\frac{3}{12}$

Ⓒ $\frac{5}{12}$

Ⓓ $\frac{6}{12}$

END OF PRACTICE SET

Common Core Mathematics

Practice Set 6

Multiple-Choice Questions

Instructions

Read each question carefully. For each multiple-choice question, fill in the circle for the correct answer.

You may use a ruler and a protractor to help you answer questions. You may not use a calculator on this test. You may also use the reference information below.

Conversions

1 mile = 5,280 feet   1 pound = 16 ounces   1 cup = 8 fluid ounces
1 mile = 1,760 yards   1 ton = 2,000 pounds   1 pint = 2 cups
1 quart = 2 pints
1 gallon = 4 quarts
1 liter = 1,000 cubic centimeters

Formulas

Right Rectangular Prism $V = Bh$ or $V = lwh$

1   The model below is made up of 1-centimeter cubes. What is a correct way to find the volume of the cube?

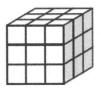

    Ⓐ   3 + 3 + 3

    Ⓑ 3^2

    Ⓒ 3^3

    Ⓓ $6(3^2)$

2   Jason is buying baseball cards. Each packet of baseball cards contains 12 baseball cards and costs $3. How many baseball cards can Jason buy for $15?

    Ⓐ   5

    Ⓑ   60

    Ⓒ   180

    Ⓓ   540

3   Which point represents the location of the ordered pair $(1\frac{1}{4}, 2\frac{1}{2})$?

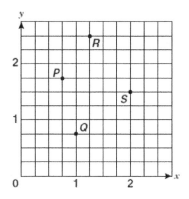

Ⓐ   Point *P*

Ⓑ   Point *Q*

Ⓒ   Point *R*

Ⓓ   Point *S*

4   Which term describes all the shapes shown below?

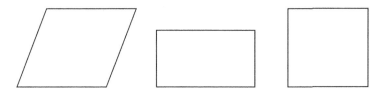

Ⓐ   Parallelogram

Ⓑ   Rectangle

Ⓒ   Rhombus

Ⓓ   Square

5   The table below shows the total cost of hiring DVDs for different numbers of DVDs.

Number of DVDs	Total Cost, in Dollars
2	6
5	15
6	18
8	24

Which equation could be used to find the total cost in dollars, c, of hiring x DVDs?

Ⓐ $c = x + 4$

Ⓑ $c = 3x$

Ⓒ $c = x + 3$

Ⓓ $c = 8x$

6   Dave bought 4 packets of pies. Three packets had 12 pies each, and one packet had 10 pies. Which number sentence shows the total number of pies Dave bought?

Ⓐ   (3 x 12) x 10

Ⓑ   (3 + 12) x 10

Ⓒ   (3 x 12) + 10

Ⓓ   (3 + 12) + 10

7   Which measurement is equivalent to 3 yards?

Ⓐ   12 feet

Ⓑ   36 feet

Ⓒ   72 inches

Ⓓ   108 inches

8   The table below shows the cost of hiring items from a hire store.

Item	Cost per Week
CD	$2
DVD	$3
Video game	$4

Which expression represents the total cost, in dollars, of hiring c CDs and d DVDs for w weeks?

Ⓐ $2c + 3d + w$

Ⓑ $w(2c + 3d)$

Ⓒ $w(2c) + 3d$

Ⓓ $2c + 3d$

9 If the numbers below were each rounded to the nearest tenth, which number would be rounded down?

   Ⓐ 17.386

   Ⓑ 35.662

   Ⓒ 23.758

   Ⓓ 76.935

10 The model below was made with 1-unit cubes.

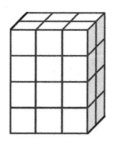

   What is the volume of the model?

   Ⓐ 12 cubic units

   Ⓑ 24 cubic units

   Ⓒ 26 cubic units

   Ⓓ 36 cubic units

11   The graph below shows a line segment with three points marked.

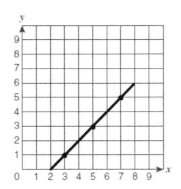

Which table shows the coordinates of these 3 points?

Ⓐ

x	1	2	3
y	3	5	7

Ⓑ

x	3	5	7
y	1	3	5

Ⓒ

x	1	3	5
y	1	2	3

Ⓓ

x	1	3	5
y	3	5	7

12   Joanne had three singing lessons one week. Two lessons went for 45 minutes, and one lesson went for 60 minutes. Which number sentence could be used to find how many minutes Joanne had singing lessons for?

    Ⓐ $2 \times (45 + 60)$

    Ⓑ $(45 + 60) \div 3$

    Ⓒ $(2 \times 45) + 60$

    Ⓓ $(2 \times 45) + (2 \times 60)$

13   How is the numeral 9.007 written in words?

    Ⓐ   Nine and seven tenths

    Ⓑ   Nine and seven thousandths

    Ⓒ   Nine and seven hundredths

    Ⓓ   Nine thousand and seven

14   The model below shows $1\frac{6}{100}$ shaded. What decimal represents the shaded part of the model?

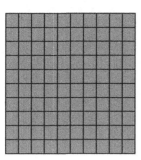 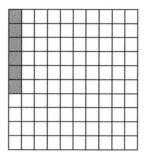

Ⓐ   1.6

Ⓑ   1.06

Ⓒ   0.16

Ⓓ   0.106

15   A rectangular toy box has a length of 90 centimeters, a width of 30 centimeters, and a height of 50 centimeters. What is the volume of the toy box?

Ⓐ   4,500 cubic centimeters

Ⓑ   6,000 cubic centimeters

Ⓒ   81,000 cubic centimeters

Ⓓ   135,000 cubic centimeters

16   A glass of water had a temperature of 25°C. Derek heated the water so that the temperature increased by 3°C every 10 minutes. What would the temperature of the water have been after 30 minutes?

Ⓐ   28°C

Ⓑ   31°C

Ⓒ   34°C

Ⓓ   37°C

17   Mr. Singh bought 2 adult zoo tickets for a total of $22, as well as 4 children's tickets. He spent $54 in total. How much was each children's ticket?

Ⓐ $8

Ⓑ $2.50

Ⓒ $9

Ⓓ $13.50

18   Emily cooked a roast on high for $1\frac{1}{2}$ hours. She then cooked it for another $1\frac{3}{4}$ hour on low. How long did she cook the roast for in all?

Ⓐ $2\frac{1}{4}$ hours

Ⓑ $2\frac{3}{4}$ hours

Ⓒ $3\frac{1}{4}$ hours

Ⓓ $3\frac{3}{4}$ hours

19   Which operation in the expression should be carried out first?

$$42 + 24 \div (3 - 1) + 5$$

  Ⓐ   42 + 24

  Ⓑ   24 ÷ 3

  Ⓒ   3 − 1

  Ⓓ   3 + 5

20   Leanne added $\frac{1}{4}$ cup of milk and $\frac{3}{8}$ cup of water to a bowl. Which diagram is shaded to show how many cups of milk and water were in the bowl in all?

Ⓐ

Ⓑ

Ⓒ

Ⓓ

21   A bulldog weighs 768 ounces. How many pounds does the bulldog weigh?

     Ⓐ   48 pounds

     Ⓑ   64 pounds

     Ⓒ   96 pounds

     Ⓓ   192 pounds

22   The cost of renting a trailer is a basic fee of $20 plus an additional $25 for each day that the trailer is rented.

Which equation can be used to find *c*, the cost in dollars of the rental for *d* days?

     Ⓐ $c = 20d + 25$

     Ⓑ $c = 25d + 20$

     Ⓒ $c = 20(d + 25)$

     Ⓓ $c = 25(d + 20)$

23 Maxwell bought a packet of 48 baseball cards. He gave 8 baseball cards to each of 4 friends. Which number sentence can be used to find the number of baseball cards Maxwell has left?

Ⓐ $(48 - 8) \times 4$

Ⓑ $(48 - 8) \div 4$

Ⓒ $48 - (8 + 4)$

Ⓓ $48 - (8 \times 4)$

24 A square garden has side lengths of $4\frac{1}{2}$ feet. What is the area of the garden? You can use the diagram below to help find the answer.

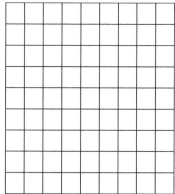

Each square is $\frac{1}{2}$ foot × $\frac{1}{2}$ foot.

Each square has an area of $\frac{1}{4}$ square feet.

Ⓐ $16\frac{1}{4}$ square feet

Ⓑ $20\frac{1}{4}$ square feet

Ⓒ $40\frac{1}{2}$ square feet

Ⓓ $182\frac{1}{4}$ square feet

25   Which two shapes have the same number of sides?

    Ⓐ   Triangle and rectangle

    Ⓑ   Rectangle and square

    Ⓒ   Hexagon and pentagon

    Ⓓ   Pentagon and triangle

26   There are 365 days in a year and 24 hours in a day. How many hours are there in a year?

    Ⓐ   8,540

    Ⓑ   8,560

    Ⓒ   8,740

    Ⓓ   8,760

27   A shape has two sides with lengths of 4 inches and two sides with lengths of 7 inches. Which of these could the shape be?

    Ⓐ   square

    Ⓑ   rectangle

    Ⓒ   rhombus

    Ⓓ   trapezoid

28   Which statement describes the value of the expression below?

$$40 \times \frac{1}{8}$$

Ⓐ   The value is greater than 40.

Ⓑ   The value is less than 40.

Ⓒ   The value is equal to 40.

Ⓓ   The value is between 0 and 1.

29   Jolie has two beakers filled with water, as shown below.

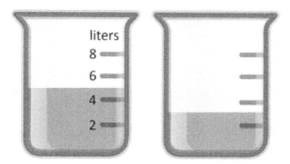

Jolie pours the smaller amount into the larger amount. How much water is in the beaker, in milliliters?

Ⓐ   6 milliliters

Ⓑ   8 milliliters

Ⓒ   6,000 milliliters

Ⓓ   8,000 milliliters

30   A baby elephant was born at a zoo. The elephant weighed 184 pounds. What is the weight, in ounces, of the elephant?

Ⓐ   1,840 ounces

Ⓑ   2,208 ounces

Ⓒ   2,944 ounces

Ⓓ   3,312 ounces

END OF PRACTICE SET

Common Core Mathematics

Practice Set 7

Short-Response and Extended-Response Questions

Instructions

Read each question carefully. Then write your answer to the question. Be sure to show your work when the question asks you to.

You may use a ruler and a protractor to help you answer questions. You may not use a calculator on this test. You may also use the reference information below.

Conversions

1 mile = 5,280 feet   1 pound = 16 ounces   1 cup = 8 fluid ounces

1 mile = 1,760 yards   1 ton = 2,000 pounds   1 pint = 2 cups

1 quart = 2 pints

1 gallon = 4 quarts

1 liter = 1,000 cubic centimeters

Formulas

Right Rectangular Prism $V = Bh$ or $V = lwh$

1   A pattern has the rule $y = 2x$. A second pattern has the rule $y = 2x + 2$. Complete the tables below to find the value of y for each value of x for the two patterns. Then plot both lines on the coordinate grid.

$y = 2x$

x	y
0	
1	
2	
3	

$y = 2x + 2$

x	y
0	
1	
2	
3	

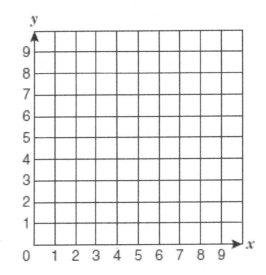

On the lines below, compare the lines on the coordinate grid.

_____

_____

_____

_____

2   A timber shelf has the measurements shown below.

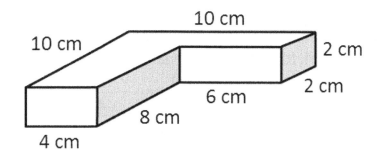

Determine **two** ways the shelf can be divided into two rectangular prisms.
Write the dimensions of the **two** sets of rectangular prisms below.

Set 1 _____ by _____ by _____

                          and

_____ by _____ by _____

Set 2 _____ by _____ by _____

                          and

_____ by _____ by _____

What is the total volume of the timber shelf? Write your answer below. Be sure to include the correct units.

_____

3   Harris and Jamie both started with no savings. Harris saved $3 per week, while Jamie saved $6 per week.

Complete the table below to show Harris's and Jamie's total savings at the end of each week for the first 6 weeks.

Week	1	2	3	4	5	6
Harris's Total Savings						
Jamie's Total Savings						

Describe the relationship between Harris's total savings and Jamie's total savings each week.

_____

_____

_____

_____

_____

4   The list below shows data a science class collected on the diameter of hailstones that fell during a storm.

Hailstone Diameter (inches)

$$\frac{1}{4}, \frac{1}{4}, \frac{1}{2}, \frac{5}{8}, \frac{1}{2}, \frac{3}{8}, \frac{5}{8}, \frac{1}{4}, \frac{7}{8}, \frac{3}{4}$$

Plot the data on the line plot below.

Hailstone Diameter (inches)

$$0 \quad \frac{1}{8} \quad \frac{1}{4} \quad \frac{3}{8} \quad \frac{1}{2} \quad \frac{5}{8} \quad \frac{3}{4} \quad \frac{7}{8} \quad 1$$

What is the difference in diameter between the largest hailstone and the smallest hailstone? Write your answer below.

_____ inches

5 Tom worked for 32 hours and earned \$448. He earned the same rate per hour.

Write an equation that can be solved to find how much Tom earns per hour. Use *h* to represent how much Tom earns per hour.

Equation _____

Solve the equation to find how much Tom earns per hour. Write your answer below.

\$ _____

6 Mitch ran 2.6 miles on Monday and 1.8 miles on Tuesday. How many miles less did Mitch run on Tuesday? Write your answer below. You can use the diagram below to find the answer.

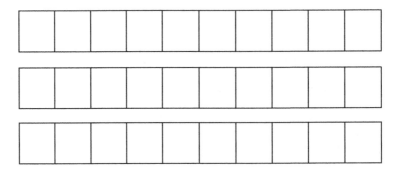

_____ miles

7   The model below is made up of 1-centimeter cubes.

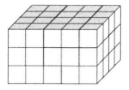

What is the volume of the model?

Show your work.

Answer _____ cubic centimeters

8   Joe made the graph below to show the locations of prizes he hid for a treasure hunt. Each star represents a treasure.

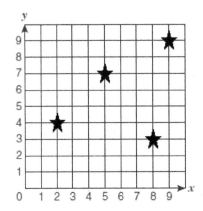

Which ordered pair represents the treasure located closest to the origin? Write your answer below.

_____

Which ordered pair represents the treasure located farthest from the origin? Write your answer below.

_____

9   Sushi sells for $3 for each small roll and $5 for each large roll. Derrick bought 4 small rolls and 7 large rolls.

Complete the expression below to show how to find the total amount Derrick spent, in dollars.

$$(\underline{} \times \underline{}) + (\underline{} \times \underline{})$$

Simplify the expression you wrote to find the total amount Derrick spent.

Answer $_____

10   There are 200 students at Kerry's elementary school. Of those students, $\frac{2}{5}$ are fifth grade students. How many fifth grade students are there?

Show your work.

Answer _____

END OF PRACTICE SET

Common Core Mathematics

Practice Set 8

Multiple-Choice Questions

Instructions

Read each question carefully. For each multiple-choice question, fill in the circle for the correct answer.

You may use a ruler and a protractor to help you answer questions. You may not use a calculator on this test. You may also use the reference information below.

Conversions

1 mile = 5,280 feet	1 pound = 16 ounces	1 cup = 8 fluid ounces
1 mile = 1,760 yards	1 ton = 2,000 pounds	1 pint = 2 cups
		1 quart = 2 pints
		1 gallon = 4 quarts
		1 liter = 1,000 cubic centimeters

Formulas

Right Rectangular Prism $V = Bh$ or $V = lwh$

1   What is the difference of 0.59 and 0.22?

Ⓐ   0.39

Ⓑ   0.37

Ⓒ   0.81

Ⓓ   0.83

2   Which procedure can be used to find the sum of the fractions?

$$1\frac{1}{3}, \ 2\frac{1}{2}, \ 3\frac{5}{6}$$

Ⓐ   Find the sum of the whole numbers, find the sum of the fractions, and then add the two sums

Ⓑ   Find the sum of the whole numbers, find the sum of the fractions, and then multiply the two sums

Ⓒ   Find the sum of the whole numbers, find the sum of the fractions, and then subtract the two sums

Ⓓ   Find the sum of the whole numbers, find the sum of the fractions, and then divide the two sums

3   Joy made 24 apple pies for a bake sale. Each serving was $\frac{1}{8}$ of a pie. How many servings did Joy make?

Ⓐ   3

Ⓑ   32

Ⓒ   96

Ⓓ   192

4   Look at the shapes and the Venn diagram below.

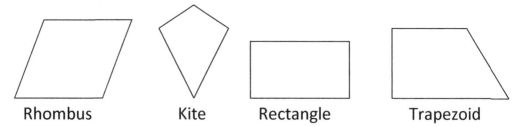

Rhombus   Kite   Rectangle   Trapezoid

At least 1 pair of parallel sides   At least 1 pair of congruent sides

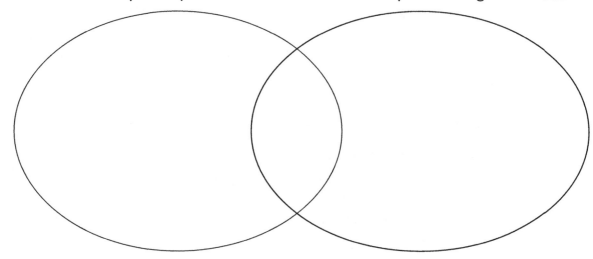

Which two shapes should be placed in the overlapping section of the Venn diagram?

Ⓐ   Rhombus and Kite

Ⓑ   Rectangle and Rhombus

Ⓒ   Kite and Rectangle

Ⓓ   Trapezoid and Kite

5   A diner has 18 tables. Each table can seat 4 people. The diner also has 8 benches that can each seat 6 people. How many people can the diner seat in all?

Ⓐ   36

Ⓑ   120

Ⓒ   260

Ⓓ   308

6   A fraction representing $\frac{6}{8}$ is shown below.

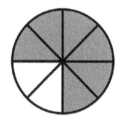

What is the value of $\frac{6}{8} \div 3$?

Ⓐ $\frac{1}{8}$

Ⓑ $\frac{3}{8}$

Ⓒ $\frac{1}{4}$

Ⓓ $\frac{3}{4}$

7   What is the value of the expression below?

$$42 + 24 \div 3 + 3$$

   Ⓐ   22

   Ⓑ   25

   Ⓒ   46

   Ⓓ   53

8   Keegan's family drinks about 2 gallons of milk every 5 days.

About how many quarts of milk does Keegan's family drink in 30 days?

   Ⓐ   24 quarts

   Ⓑ   48 quarts

   Ⓒ   240 quarts

   Ⓓ   300 quarts

9 Chan spent $\frac{3}{8}$ of his total homework time completing his science homework. What calculation could be used to convert the fraction to a decimal?

Ⓐ $3 \div 8 \times 100$

Ⓑ $8 \div 3 \times 100$

Ⓒ $3 \div 8$

Ⓓ $8 \div 3$

10 A recipe for pancakes requires $2\frac{2}{3}$ cups of flour. Donna only has $1\frac{1}{2}$ cups of flour. How many more cups of flour does Donna need?

Ⓐ $\frac{1}{3}$ cup

Ⓑ $\frac{1}{6}$ cup

Ⓒ $1\frac{1}{3}$ cups

Ⓓ $1\frac{1}{6}$ cups

11 There are 6 reams of paper in a box. There are 144 boxes of paper on a pallet. How many reams of paper are on a pallet?

Ⓐ   24

Ⓑ   576

Ⓒ   644

Ⓓ   864

12   Byron made 9 baskets out of 15 baskets he attempted. What fraction of his baskets did he make?

Ⓐ $\dfrac{1}{3}$

Ⓑ $\dfrac{1}{6}$

Ⓒ $\dfrac{3}{5}$

Ⓓ $\dfrac{3}{10}$

13   The mass of a car is 1.56 tons. What is the mass of the car in pounds?

Ⓐ   312 pounds

Ⓑ   3,120 pounds

Ⓒ   31,200 pounds

Ⓓ   312,000 pounds

14   The table below shows a set of number pairs. Which equation shows the relationship between x and y?

x	y
1	1
3	5
5	9

Ⓐ $y = x + 2$

Ⓑ $y = x + 4$

Ⓒ $y = 2x - 1$

Ⓓ $y = 3x - 4$

15 Leonard bought 12 tickets to a charity event. The total cost of the tickets was $216. The expression below can be used to find the cost of each ticket.

$$216 \div 12$$

Which of the following is equivalent to the above expression?

Ⓐ $(240 \div 12) + (24 \div 12)$

Ⓑ $(200 \div 10) + (16 \div 2)$

Ⓒ $(216 \div 10) + (216 \div 2)$

Ⓓ $(120 \div 12) + (96 \div 12)$

16 Which term does NOT describe the figure below?

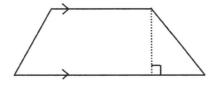

Ⓐ   Parallelogram

Ⓑ   Polygon

Ⓒ   Quadrilateral

Ⓓ   Trapezoid

17   Which point is located at (6, 3)?

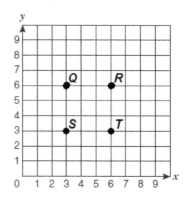

Ⓐ   Point *Q*

Ⓑ   Point *R*

Ⓒ   Point *S*

Ⓓ   Point *T*

18   The table below shows the relationship between the original price and the sale price of a book.

Original price, P	Sale price, S
$10	$7.50
$12	$9
$14	$10.50
$16	$12

What is the rule to find the sale price of a book, in dollars?

Ⓐ $S = 0.25P$

Ⓑ $S = 0.75P$

Ⓒ $S = P - 2.5$

Ⓓ $S = P - 7.5$

19   Leo measures the length, width, and height of a block. He multiplies the length, width, and height. What is Leo finding?

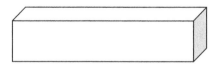

Ⓐ   Surface area

Ⓑ   Mass

Ⓒ   Volume

Ⓓ   Perimeter

20   Which figure below does NOT have any parallel sides?

21   The cost of renting a windsurfer is a basic fee of $15 plus an additional $5 for each hour that the windsurfer is rented. Which equation can be used to find c, the cost in dollars of the rental for h hours?

Ⓐ $c = 15h + 5$

Ⓑ $c = 5h + 15$

Ⓒ $c = 15(h + 5)$

Ⓓ $c = 5(h + 15)$

22   The graph below shows the line segment *PQ*. Point *P* is at (3, 9). Point *Q* is at (3, 1).

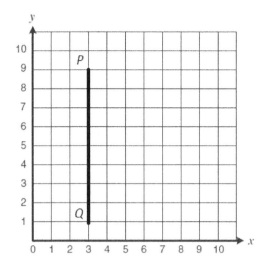

What is the length of the line segment *PQ*?

Ⓐ   6 units

Ⓑ   8 units

Ⓒ   9 units

Ⓓ   10 units

23   What decimal is equivalent to the fraction $\frac{33}{100}$?

Ⓐ   0.033

Ⓑ   0.33

Ⓒ   33.0

Ⓓ   3.3

24   Which decimal is represented below?

$$(4 \times 100) + (8 \times 1) + (6 \times \frac{1}{100}) + (3 \times \frac{1}{1000})$$

   Ⓐ   480.63

   Ⓑ   480.063

   Ⓒ   408.63

   Ⓓ   408.063

25   If $p = 5$, what is the value of $4(p + 7)$?

   Ⓐ   16

   Ⓑ   27

   Ⓒ   48

   Ⓓ   64

26   Which expression can represent 4 less than the quotient of 192 and 3?

   Ⓐ $(192 \times 3) - 4$

   Ⓑ $(192 \div 3) - 4$

   Ⓒ $4 - (192 \times 3)$

   Ⓓ $4 - (192 \div 3)$

27   The volume of a single layer in a rectangular prism is 24 cubic centimeters. There are 4 layers in the rectangular prism. What is the volume, in cubic centimeters, of this rectangular prism?

Ⓐ   6

Ⓑ   20

Ⓒ   28

Ⓓ   96

28   Which expression represents the situation below?

the number of $\frac{1}{4}$-cup peanut cups that can be filled by 6 cups of peanuts

Ⓐ $\frac{1}{4} + 6$

Ⓑ $\frac{1}{4} \times 6$

Ⓒ $6 - \frac{1}{4}$

Ⓓ $6 \div \frac{1}{4}$

29   What decimal is equivalent to $\frac{87}{100}$?

   Ⓐ   0.87

   Ⓑ   8.70

   Ⓒ   87.100

   Ⓓ   100.87

30   Which expression could be represented by the shaded parts of the model below?

   Ⓐ $\frac{3}{4} + \frac{1}{5}$

   Ⓑ $\frac{3}{4} \times \frac{1}{5}$

   Ⓒ $\frac{3}{4} + 5$

   Ⓓ $\frac{3}{4} \times 5$

END OF PRACTICE SET

Common Core Mathematics

Practice Set 9

Multiple-Choice Questions

Instructions

Read each question carefully. For each multiple-choice question, fill in the circle for the correct answer.

You may use a ruler and a protractor to help you answer questions. You may not use a calculator on this test. You may also use the reference information below.

Conversions

1 mile = 5,280 feet	1 pound = 16 ounces	1 cup = 8 fluid ounces
1 mile = 1,760 yards	1 ton = 2,000 pounds	1 pint = 2 cups
		1 quart = 2 pints
		1 gallon = 4 quarts
		1 liter = 1,000 cubic centimeters

Formulas

Right Rectangular Prism $V = Bh$ or $V = lwh$

1   Liam drew a triangle with no equal side lengths, as shown below.

What type of triangle did Liam draw?

Ⓐ   Scalene

Ⓑ   Equilateral

Ⓒ   Isosceles

Ⓓ   Right

2   The table below shows the total number of lemons in different numbers of
       bags of lemons.

Number of Bags (B)	Number of Lemons (L)
2	16
3	24
5	40
8	64

What is the relationship between the number of bags, B, and the total
number of lemons, L?

Ⓐ $L = 16B$

Ⓑ $L = B \times B$

Ⓒ $L = B + 8$

Ⓓ $L = 8B$

3   Amy ordered 3 pizzas for \$6.95 each. She also bought a soft drink for \$1.95. Which equation can be used to find how much change, c, she should receive from \$30?

    Ⓐ $c = 30 - 3(6.95 + 1.95)$

    Ⓑ $c = 30 - 3(6.95 - 1.95)$

    Ⓒ $c = 30 - 6.95 - 1.95$

    Ⓓ $c = 30 - (6.95 \times 3) - 1.95$

4   What is the decimal 55.146 rounded to the nearest tenth?

    Ⓐ   55.1

    Ⓑ   55.2

    Ⓒ   55.14

    Ⓓ   55.15

5   What is the value of the expression below?

$$28 + 4 \div 2 + (9 - 5)$$

    Ⓐ   20

    Ⓑ   30

    Ⓒ   34

    Ⓓ   44

6 The table shows the side length of a rhombus and the perimeter of a rhombus.

Side Length, x (cm)	Perimeter, y (cm)
1	4
2	8
3	12
4	16

Which equation represents the relationship between side length and perimeter?

 Ⓐ $y = x + 3$

 Ⓑ $y = 4x$

 Ⓒ $x = y + 4$

 Ⓓ $x = 4y$

7 A florist sells balloons in sets of 6. A customer ordered several sets of 6 balloons. Which of these could be the total number of balloons ordered?

 Ⓐ 48

 Ⓑ 50

 Ⓒ 52

 Ⓓ 56

8   The table shows the amount of Don's phone bill for four different months.

Month	Amount
April	$12.22
May	$12.09
June	$12.18
July	$12.05

In which month did Don spend the least on phone calls?

Ⓐ   April

Ⓑ   May

Ⓒ   June

Ⓓ   July

9   Marcus sold drinks at a lemonade stand. The table shows how many drinks of each size he sold.

Size	Number Sold
Small	15
Medium	20
Large	5
Extra large	10

Which size drink made up $\frac{3}{10}$ of the total sold?

Ⓐ   Small

Ⓑ   Medium

Ⓒ   Large

Ⓓ   Extra large

10   What is the rule to find the value of a term in the sequence below?

Position, n	Value of Term
1	3
2	5
3	7
4	9

Ⓐ $4n - 4$

Ⓑ $3n$

Ⓒ $2n + 1$

Ⓓ $n + 2$

11   The table shows the amount of rainfall for the first four days of May.

Date	1st	2nd	3rd	4th
Rainfall (cm)	4.59	4.43	4.50	4.61

Which day had the lowest rainfall?

Ⓐ   1st

Ⓑ   2nd

Ⓒ   3rd

Ⓓ   4th

12   What value for *x* makes the equation below true?

$$54 \div x = 9$$

(A)   6

(B)   7

(C)   8

(D)   9

13   The grid below represents 4 x 7.

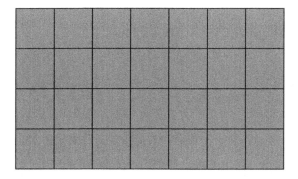

Which of these is another way to represent 4 x 7?

(A)   7 + 7 + 7 + 7

(B)   7 + 7 + 7 + 7 + 7 + 7 + 7

(C)   4 + 4 + 4 + 4

(D)   4 x 4 x 4 x 4

14   Sandy has 129 dimes. Marvin has 185 dimes. What is the total value of Sandy and Marvin's dimes?

Ⓐ $3.04

Ⓑ $3.14

Ⓒ $30.40

Ⓓ $31.40

15   Which of the following is a correct definition of a square?

Ⓐ   A rectangle with two pairs of parallel sides

Ⓑ   A rectangle with adjacent sides perpendicular

Ⓒ   A rhombus with four equal sides

Ⓓ   A rhombus with four right angles

16   Ellen multiplies the number 3 by a fraction. The result is a number greater than 3. Which of these could be the fraction?

Ⓐ $1\frac{1}{4}$

Ⓑ $\frac{8}{9}$

Ⓒ $\frac{1}{6}$

Ⓓ $\frac{1}{2}$

17   Look at the two sequences of numbers below.

> First sequence: 0, 4, 8, 12, 16, 20, 24, ...
> Second sequence: 0, 8, 16, 24, 32, 40, 48, ...

If the 100th term in the first sequence is represented as n, which of these gives the 100th term in the second sequence?

Ⓐ $n + 4$

Ⓑ $n + 8$

Ⓒ $2n$

Ⓓ $2n + 4$

18   Lloyd bought 4 T-shirts. Each T-shirt cost $7. Which is one way to work out how much change Lloyd would receive from $30?

Ⓐ   Add 4 to 7 and subtract the result from 30

Ⓑ   Add 4 to 7 and add the result to 30

Ⓒ   Multiply 4 by 7 and add the result to 30

Ⓓ   Multiply 4 by 7 and subtract the result from 30

19   An Italian restaurant sells four types of meals. The owner made this table to show how many meals of each type were sold one night. According to the table, which statement is true?

Meal	Number Sold
Pasta	16
Pizza	18
Salad	11
Risotto	9

Ⓐ   The store sold more pizza meals than salad and risotto meals combined.

Ⓑ   The store sold twice as many pizza meals as risotto meals.

Ⓒ   The store sold more pasta meals than any other type of meal.

Ⓓ   The store sold half as many salad meals as pasta meals.

20   Jordan is putting CDs in a case. She can fit 24 CDs in each row. She has 120 CDs. Which equation can be used to find the total number of rows, r, she can fill?

Ⓐ $r \times 120 = 24$

Ⓑ $r \div 24 = 120$

Ⓒ $120 \times 24 = r$

Ⓓ $120 \div 24 = r$

21 Jay made 8 trays of 6 muffins each.

He gave 12 muffins away. He packed the remaining muffins in bags of 4 muffins each. Which expression can be used to find how many bags of muffins he packed?

Ⓐ $(8 \times 6) - 12 \div 4$

Ⓑ $(8 \times 6) - (12 \div 4)$

Ⓒ $8 \times (6 - 12 \div 4)$

Ⓓ $(8 \times 6 - 12) \div 4$

22 The table shows the side length of an equilateral triangle and the perimeter of an equilateral triangle.

Side Length, l (inches)	Perimeter, P (inches)
2	6
3	9
4	12
5	15

Which equation represents the relationship between side length and perimeter?

Ⓐ $P = l + 4$

Ⓑ $P = 3l$

Ⓒ $l = P + 4$

Ⓓ $l = 3P$

23   Which term describes the triangle below?

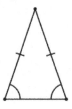

- Ⓐ   Isosceles

- Ⓑ   Scalene

- Ⓒ   Equilateral

- Ⓓ   Right

24   Which of these is equal to 600,000?

- Ⓐ   60 thousands

- Ⓑ   60 ten-thousands

- Ⓒ   60 hundred-thousands

- Ⓓ   60 millions

25   Which statement is true about the product of $\frac{1}{3}$ and 6?

- Ⓐ   The product is greater than 6.

- Ⓑ   The product is less than $\frac{1}{3}$.

- Ⓒ   The product is a value between the two factors.

- Ⓓ   The product is a value equal to one of the factors.

26 Leon drew a polygon in which exactly one angle was a right angle. What kind of polygon could he have drawn?

Ⓐ   trapezoid

Ⓑ   rhombus

Ⓒ   square

Ⓓ   rectangle

27 Helen makes 120 fluid ounces of lemonade. She sells the lemonade for $2 per bottle. Each bottle holds 1 cup of lemonade. How much will Helen make if she sells all the lemonade?

Ⓐ $10

Ⓑ $15

Ⓒ $20

Ⓓ $30

28   Zachary builds a cube from 1-cm unit cubes and then removes some unit cubes from the front of the cube, as shown below.

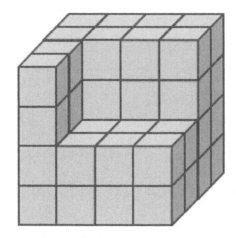

What is the volume of the figure remaining?

Ⓐ   52 cubic centimeters

Ⓑ   55 cubic centimeters

Ⓒ   58 cubic centimeters

Ⓓ   64 cubic centimeters

29   How many $\frac{1}{4}$-cup servings are in 5 cups?

Ⓐ $\frac{1}{20}$

Ⓑ $1\frac{1}{4}$

Ⓒ   9

Ⓓ   20

30 Wyatt made the grid below to show the locations of his home, w, and the locations of his friends.

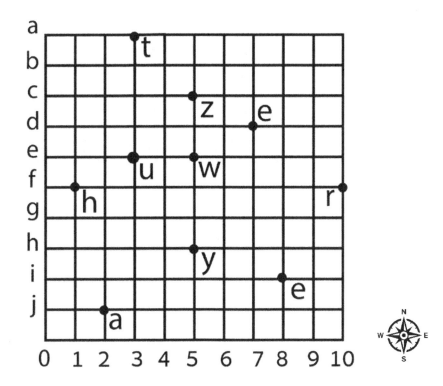

Which friend could Wyatt visit by travelling directly south without making any turns?

Ⓐ   Zoe, represented by z

Ⓑ   Hank, represented by h

Ⓒ   Ursula, represented by u

Ⓓ   Yvonne, represented by y

END OF PRACTICE SET

Common Core Mathematics

Practice Test 10

Short-Response and Extended-Response Questions

Instructions

Read each question carefully. Then write your answer to the question. Be sure to show your work when the question asks you to.

You may use a ruler and a protractor to help you answer questions. You may not use a calculator on this test. You may also use the reference information below.

Conversions

1 mile = 5,280 feet	1 pound = 16 ounces	1 cup = 8 fluid ounces
1 mile = 1,760 yards	1 ton = 2,000 pounds	1 pint = 2 cups
		1 quart = 2 pints
		1 gallon = 4 quarts
		1 liter = 1,000 cubic centimeters

Formulas

Right Rectangular Prism $V = Bh$ or $V = lwh$

1   Bradley has 64 1-inch cubic blocks. He uses all the blocks to build a rectangular prism that is 2 inches high and 2 inches wide. How long is the rectangular prism? Write your answer below.

_____ inches

Complete the table below to show the dimensions of **two** other rectangular prisms Bradley could make using all the blocks.

	Rectangular Prism 1	Rectangular Prism 2
Length		
Height		
Width		

Could Bradley use all the blocks to make a cube? Explain your answer.

_____

_____

_____

_____

2   A pattern has the rule $y = 3x + 1$. Complete the table below to find the value of y for each value of x.

x	y
0	
1	
2	
3	

Plot the points from the table on the coordinate grid below and draw the line that connects the points.

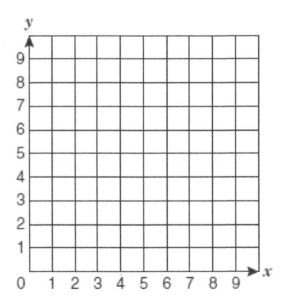

3   The grid below represents Roberto's backyard.

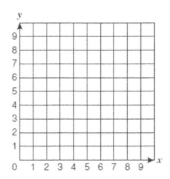

A lemon tree is located at the point (6, 5). An orange tree is located 2 units to the right and 3 units up from the lemon tree. Find the coordinates that represent the location of the orange tree. Write the coordinates below.

_____

Explain how you found your answer.

_____

_____

_____

_____

4   Look at the figure below.

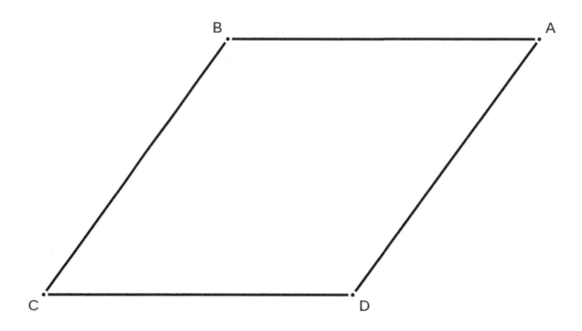

Identify the two pairs of parallel line segments. Write each line segment on one of the lines below.

_____ and _____, _____ and _____

Name the shape and describe the properties you used to identify it.

_____

_____

_____

_____

5   The statements below describe quadrilaterals.

At least 1 pair of parallel sides

2 pairs of perpendicular sides

4 equal angles

4 right angles

4 congruent sides

Circle the statement that correctly describes a trapezoid.

Which statement above could be used to tell the difference between a rectangle and a square? Explain your answer.

_____

_____

_____

_____

_____

6 A restaurant manager kept a record of the pieces of pie sold one week. He made this list to show the results.

- $\frac{1}{4}$ of the pieces sold were apple pie
- $\frac{3}{8}$ of the pieces sold were pumpkin pie
- $\frac{1}{12}$ of the pieces sold were cherry pie
- The rest of the pieces sold were peach pie.

Part A

What fraction of the pieces sold were peach pie?

Show your work.

Answer _____

Part B

If there were a total of 360 pieces of pie sold that week, how many pieces of cherry pie were sold?

Show your work.

Answer _____

7   Karen made this table to show the amount she spent on lunch each day one week.

Day	Amount
Monday	$5.73
Tuesday	$5.49
Wednesday	$5.51
Thursday	$5.27
Friday	$5.80

What is the total amount Karen spent on lunch that week?

Show your work.

Answer _____

8   Plot the number 3.8 on the number line below.

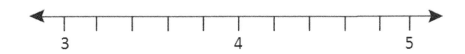

What is 3.8 rounded to the nearest whole number? Write your answer below.

_____

9   Circle the measurements that are equivalent to 600 centimeters.

0.6 mm   6 mm   60 mm   6000 mm

0.6 m   6 m   60 m   6000 m

Convert 600 centimeters to kilometers. Write your answer below.

_____ kilometers

10   The model below is made up of 1-centimeter cubes.

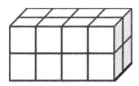

Write and solve an equation to find the volume of the model.

Answer _____ cubic centimeters

If the height of the model is doubled, how does the volume of the model change? Explain your answer.

_____

_____

_____

_____

END OF PRACTICE SET

ANSWER KEY

Mathematics Learning Standards

In 2017, the state of New York introduced the Next Generation Learning Standards. These are revised standards that replace the previous Common Core Learning Standards, though remain very close in content. State testing will continue to assess the Common Core Learning Standards until 2020, but the new standards will be gradually implemented over this time. This workbook has aligned all questions to the new Next Generation Learning Standards. However, the questions still also cover the Common Core standards that are assessed on the state tests.

Assessing Skills and Knowledge

The skills listed in the Next Generation Learning Standards are divided into five topics, or domains. These are:

- Operations and Algebraic Thinking
- Number and Operations in Base Ten
- Number and Operations – Fractions
- Measurement and Data
- Geometry

The answer key identifies the topic for each question. Use the topics listed to identify general areas of strength and weakness. Then target revision and instruction accordingly.

The answer key also identifies the specific math skill that each question is testing. Use the skills listed to identify skills that the student is lacking. Then target revision and instruction accordingly.

Scoring Short-Response and Extended-Response Questions

This practice test book includes short-response and extended-response questions, where students provide a written answer to a question or complete a task. These questions are often scored based on the final answer given as well as the work shown. When asked to show work, students may show calculations, use diagrams, or explain their thinking or process in words. Any form of work that shows the student's understanding can be accepted. Other questions are scored based on tasks completed, explanations given, or justifications given. Answers are provided for these questions, as well as guidance on how to score the questions.

Common Core Mathematics, Practice Set 1

Question	Answer	Topic	Next Generation Learning Standard
1	C	Geometry	Use a pair of perpendicular number lines, called axes, to define a coordinate system, with the intersection of the lines (the origin) arranged to coincide with the 0 on each line and a given point in the plane located by using an ordered pair of numbers, called its coordinates.
2	0.08	Number & Operations in Base Ten	Add, subtract, multiply, and divide decimals to hundredths, using concrete models or drawings.
3	D	Measurement & Data	Recognize volume as an attribute of solid figures and understand concepts of volume measurement.
4	B	Geometry	Represent real world and mathematical problems by graphing points in the first quadrant of the coordinate plane, and interpret coordinate values of points in the context of the situation.
5	>, <, >, >, =, <	Number & Operations in Base Ten	Compare two decimals to thousandths based on meanings of the digits in each place, using >, =, and < symbols to record the results of comparisons.
6	See Below	Number & Operations in Base Ten	Add, subtract, multiply, and divide decimals to hundredths.
7	See Below	Operations/Algebraic Thinking	Generate two numerical patterns using two given rules. Identify apparent relationships between corresponding terms. Form ordered pairs consisting of corresponding terms from the two patterns, and graph the ordered pairs on a coordinate plane.
8	See Below	Measurement & Data	Find the volume of a right rectangular prism with whole-number side lengths by packing it with unit cubes, and show that the volume is the same as would be found by multiplying the edge lengths, equivalently by multiplying the height by the area of the base.
9	See Below	Number & Operations in Base Ten	Recognize that in a multi-digit number, a digit in one place represents 10 times as much as it represents in the place to its right and 1/10 of what it represents in the place to its left.
10	See Below	Geometry	Classify two-dimensional figures in a hierarchy based on properties.

Q6.
$3.20

The work should show the calculation 12.8 ÷ 4 = 3.2.

Scoring Information
Give a total score out of 2.
Give a score of 1 for the correct answer.
Give a score out of 1 for the working.

Q7.
The first table should be completed with the *y* values 0, 1, 2, and 3.
The second table should be completed with the *y* values 2, 3, 4, and 5.
The two lines should be graphed as shown below.

The student should give a reasonable comparison of the lines. The comparison should include that the lines are parallel and that the second line is 2 units above the first line.

Scoring Information
Give a total score out of 3.
Give a score of 0.5 for each table correctly completed.
Give a score of 0.5 for each line correctly graphed.
Give a score out of 1 for the comparison of the lines.

Q8.
680

The work could show the calculation of 4 × 10 × 17 = 680. The work may also show calculating 4 rows of 170 cubes or 17 rows of 40 cubes.

Scoring Information
Give a total score out of 2.
Give a score of 1 for the correct answer.
Give a score out of 1 for the working.

Q9.
3,000 hundreds
300 thousands
30 ten-thousands
3 hundred-thousands

Scoring Information
Give a total score out of 2.
Give a score of 0.5 for each correct answer.

Q10.
Circle for "4 equal sides": rhombus
Circle for "4 right angles": rectangle
Overlapping circles: square

Scoring Information
Give a total score out of 3.
Give a score of 1 for each shape correctly placed.

Common Core Mathematics, Practice Set 2

Question	Answer	Topic	Next Generation Learning Standard
1	D	Geometry	Use a pair of perpendicular number lines, called axes, to define a coordinate system. Understand that the first number indicates how far to travel from the origin in the direction of one axis, and the second number indicates how far to travel in the direction of the second axis.
2	D	Number & Operations in Base Ten	Compare two decimals to thousandths based on meanings of the digits in each place.
3	A	Measurement & Data	Find the volume of a right rectangular prism with whole-number side lengths by packing it with unit cubes, and show that the volume is the same as would be found by multiplying the edge lengths.
4	0.2 ÷ 4 0.05	Number & Operations in Base Ten	Add, subtract, multiply, and divide decimals to hundredths, using concrete models or drawings.
5	3rd, 5th, and 6th	Number & Operations-Fractions	Use benchmark fractions and number sense of fractions to estimate mentally and assess the reasonableness of answers.
6	(220 − 90) ÷ 5 26	Operations/Algebraic Thinking	Apply the order of operations to evaluate numerical expressions.
7	See Below	Number & Operations in Base Ten	Perform operations with multi-digit whole numbers and with decimals to hundredths.
8	See Below	Measurement & Data	Make a line plot to display a data set of measurements in fractions of a unit (1/2, 1/4, 1/8). Use operations on fractions for this grade to solve problems involving information presented in line plots.
9	See Below	Geometry	Represent real world and mathematical problems by graphing points in the first quadrant of the coordinate plane.
10	See Below	Geometry	Classify two-dimensional figures in a hierarchy based on properties.

Q7.
2,700
$14,850
64,800 fluid ounces
4,050 pints

Scoring Information
Give a total score out of 2.
Give a score of 0.5 for each correct answer.

Q8.
The line plot should be completed as shown below.

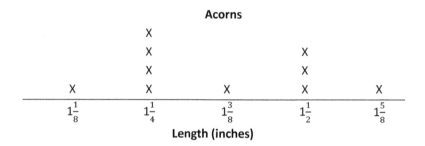

Answer: $\frac{1}{2}$ inches

Scoring Information
Give a total score out of 3.
Give a score out of 2 for the line plot.
Give a score of 1 for the correct answer.

Q9.
The table should be completed with the y values 2, 4, 6, and 8.
The line should be graphed as shown below.

Scoring Information
Give a total score out of 2.
Give a score of 1 for the table correctly completed.
Give a score of 1 for the line correctly graphed.

Q10.
Circle for "At least 1 pair of parallel sides": Trapezoid
Circle for "At least 1 pair of congruent sides": Kite
Overlapping circles: Rectangle, Square

Scoring Information
Give a total score out of 2.
Give a score of 0.5 for each shape correctly placed.

Common Core Mathematics, Practice Set 3

Question	Answer	Topic	Next Generation Learning Standard
1	A	Number & Operations in Base Ten	Perform operations with multi-digit whole numbers.
2	D	Geometry	Represent real world and mathematical problems by graphing points in the first quadrant of the coordinate plane, and interpret coordinate values of points in the context of the situation.
3	B	Number & Operations-Fractions	Interpret a fraction as division of the numerator by the denominator.
4	D	Geometry	Classify two-dimensional figures in a hierarchy based on properties.
5	C	Number & Operations in Base Ten	Find whole-number quotients of whole numbers with up to four-digit dividends and two-digit divisors, using strategies based on properties of operations.
6	B	Number & Operations in Base Ten	Find whole-number quotients of whole numbers. Illustrate and explain the calculation by using equations, rectangular arrays, and/or area models.
7	C	Operations/Algebraic Thinking	Write simple expressions that record calculations with numbers, and interpret numerical expressions without evaluating them.
8	See Below	Number & Operations in Base Ten	Perform operations with multi-digit whole numbers. Fluently multiply multi-digit whole numbers using a standard algorithm.
9	See Below	Operations/Algebraic Thinking	Apply the order of operations to evaluate numerical expressions.
10	See Below	Measurement & Data	Convert among different-sized standard measurement units within a given measurement system, and use these conversions in solving multi-step, real world problems.
11	See Below	Number & Operations-Fractions	Solve word problems involving addition and subtraction of fractions referring to the same whole, including cases of unlike denominators.
12	See Below	Number & Operations in Base Ten	Add, subtract, multiply, and divide decimals to hundredths.
13	See Below	Number & Operations in Base Ten	Add, subtract, multiply, and divide decimals to hundredths.
14	See Below	Geometry	Represent real world and mathematical problems by graphing points in the first quadrant of the coordinate plane, and interpret coordinate values of points in the context of the situation.
15	See Below	Geometry	Classify two-dimensional figures in a hierarchy based on properties.
16	C	Operations/Algebraic Thinking	Analyze patterns and relationships by identifying apparent relationships between corresponding terms.
17	A	Geometry	Classify two-dimensional figures in a hierarchy based on properties.
18	D	Number & Operations-Fractions	Solve word problems involving addition and subtraction of fractions referring to the same whole, including cases of unlike denominators.

| 19 | C | Number & Operations in Base Ten | Add, subtract, multiply, and divide decimals to hundredths. |
| 20 | D | Operations/Algebraic Thinking | Apply the order of operations to evaluate numerical expressions. |

Q8.
33

The work should show the calculation of $(48 \times 7) - 303 = 33$.

Scoring Information
Give a total score out of 2.
Give a score of 1 for the correct answer.
Give a score out of 1 for the working.

Q9.
34

The work should show the following steps.
$(16 + 20) - 8 \div 4 \rightarrow (36) - 8 \div 4 \rightarrow (36) - 2 \rightarrow 34$

Scoring Information
Give a total score out of 2.
Give a score of 1 for the correct answer.
Give a score out of 1 for the working.

Q10.
5 pints

The work should show the conversion of 3 quarts to 6 pints, and then the subtraction of 1 pint.

Scoring Information
Give a total score out of 2.
Give a score of 1 for the correct answer.
Give a score out of 1 for the working.

Q11.
$6\frac{1}{4}$ minutes

The work may show a numerical calculation of $100 \div 16$, or may use the grid to divide 100 into 16 segments with 4 squares remaining or groups of 16 segments with 4 squares remaining.

Scoring Information
Give a total score out of 2.
Give a score of 1 for the correct answer.
Give a score out of 1 for the working.

Q12.
973.2 miles

The work should show the calculation of 8192.6 – 7219.4 = 973.2.

Scoring Information
Give a total score out of 2.
Give a score of 1 for the correct answer.
Give a score out of 1 for the working.

Q13.
$0.55 or 55 cents

The work should show the calculation of (1.85 + 0.95) – 2.25 = 0.55.

Scoring Information
Give a total score out of 2.
Give a score of 1 for the correct answer.
Give a score out of 1 for the working.

Q14.
(9, 1)

The student may describe the calculation (5 + 4, 4 – 3) = (9, 1), or may describe plotting the new point on the grid and reading the coordinates.

Scoring Information
Give a total score out of 3.
Give a score of 1 for the correct answer.
Give a score out of 2 for the explanation.

Q15.
isosceles

The student should explain that the triangle has two sides of equal length and one side of a different length.

Scoring Information
Give a total score out of 3.
Give a score of 1 for the correct answer.
Give a score out of 2 for the explanation.

Common Core Mathematics, Practice Set 4

Question	Answer	Topic	Next Generation Learning Standard
1	See Below	Number & Operations-Fractions	Solve word problems involving addition and subtraction of fractions referring to the same whole, including cases of unlike denominators.
2	C	Number & Operations-Fractions	Solve word problems involving division of whole numbers leading to answers in the form of fractions.
3	B	Measurement & Data	Convert among different-sized standard measurement units within a given measurement system.
4	B	Number & Operations-Fractions	Add and subtract fractions with unlike denominators.
5	A	Number & Operations in Base Ten	Compare two decimals to thousandths based on meanings of the digits in each place, using >, =, and < symbols to record the results of comparisons.
6	C	Operations/Algebraic Thinking	Form ordered pairs consisting of corresponding terms from the two patterns, and graph the ordered pairs on a coordinate plane.
7	B	Operations/Algebraic Thinking	Analyze patterns and relationships by identifying apparent relationships between corresponding terms.
8	See Below	Number & Operations in Base Ten	Find whole-number quotients of whole numbers with up to four-digit dividends and two-digit divisors.
9	See Below	Number & Operations in Base Ten	Add, subtract, multiply, and divide decimals to hundredths.
10	See Below	Measurement & Data	Measure volumes by counting unit cubes, using cubic cm, cubic in., cubic ft., and improvised units.
11	See Below	Geometry	Locate a point in a coordinate system by using an ordered pair of numbers, called its coordinates. Understand the convention that the names of the two axes and the coordinates correspond.
12	See Below	Number & Operations-Fractions	Find the area of a rectangle with fractional side lengths by tiling it with rectangles of the appropriate unit fraction side lengths, and show that the area is the same as would be found by multiplying the side lengths. Multiply fractional side lengths to find areas of rectangles, and represent fraction products as rectangular areas.
13	See Below	Number & Operations-Fractions	Apply and extend previous understandings of multiplication to multiply a fraction by a fraction.
14	See Below	Number & Operations-Fractions	Apply and extend previous understandings of division to divide unit fractions by whole numbers and whole numbers by unit fractions.
15	See Below	Number & Operations in Base Ten	Recognize that in a multi-digit number, a digit in one place represents 10 times as much as it represents in the place to its right and 1/10 of what it represents in the place to its left.
16	C	Number & Operations in Base Ten	Read and write decimals to thousandths using base-ten numerals, number names, and expanded form.
17	B	Number & Operations-Fractions	Solve real world problems involving multiplication of fractions and mixed numbers.
18	C	Measurement & Data	Convert among different-sized standard measurement units within a given measurement system.
19	C	Number & Operations in Base Ten	Use whole-number exponents to denote powers of 10.
20	D	Number & Operations in Base Ten	Explain patterns in the placement of the decimal point when a decimal is multiplied or divided by a power of 10.

Q1.
The diagram should be shaded as shown below.

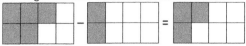

Answer: $\frac{3}{8}$

Scoring Information
Give a total score out of 2.
Give a score out of 1 for the shading.
Give a score of 1 for the correct answer.

Q8.
16

The work may show the calculation of 192 ÷ 12 = 16. The work could also show a diagram representing 16 rows of 12.

Scoring Information
Give a total score out of 2.
Give a score of 1 for the correct answer.
Give a score out of 1 for the working.

Q9.
$2.60

The work could show the calculation of 20 – (14.85 + 2.55) = 2.60 or could show the two-step subtraction of 20 – 14.85 = 5.15 and 5.15 – 2.55 = 2.60.

Scoring Information
Give a total score out of 2.
Give a score of 1 for the correct answer.
Give a score out of 1 for the working.

Q10.
24 cubic inches

The work may show the calculation 3 × 1 × 8 = 24. The work may also show counting 3 rows of 8 or 8 columns of 3.

Scoring Information
Give a total score out of 2.
Give a score of 1 for the correct answer.
Give a score out of 1 for the working.

Q11.
Part A
The student should complete the table as shown below.

x	0	2	4
y	8	5	2

Part B
(0, 8)

Scoring Information
Give a total score out of 2.
Give a score of 1 for the correct answer to Part A.
Give a score of 1 for the correct answer to Part B.

Q12.
The diagram should be shaded to show a 3 × 3 section, as shown. The student should recognize that 9 out of 16 squares are shaded, so the area is $\frac{9}{16}$ square feet.

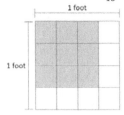

Area: $\frac{9}{16}$ square feet

Scoring Information
Give a total score out of 3.
Give a score out of 2 for shading the diagram.
Give a score of 1 for the correct answer.

Q13.
$\frac{1}{6}$

The student may find the fraction with blue stars as $\frac{1}{2} \times \frac{1}{3} = \frac{1}{6}$. The student may also use a diagram such as the one below.

Yellow	Yellow	Yellow
Blue, stars	Blue, no stars	Blue, no stars

Scoring Information
Give a total score out of 2.
Give a score of 1 for the correct answer.
Give a score out of 1 for the working.

Q14.
The model should have 14 squares shaded.
Answer: $\frac{7}{10}$

The student should describe using half of the shaded squares to represent $1\frac{2}{5} \div 2$, and seeing on the diagram that this is equal to 7 of the 10 squares. The student could also describe adding half of the whole number 1 to half of the fraction $\frac{2}{5}$.

Scoring Information
Give a total score out of 3.
Give a score of 1 for the correct shading.
Give a score of 1 for the correct answer.
Give a score out of 1 for the explanation.

Q15.
257 and 275

The explanation should refer to the place value of the numbers. It may describe how the number with the lowest value should be in the hundreds place.

Scoring Information
Give a total score out of 3.
Give a score of 1 for each correct number.
Give a score out of 1 for the explanation.

Common Core Mathematics, Practice Set 5

Question	Answer	Topic	Next Generation Learning Standard
1	C	Number & Operations-Fractions	Add and subtract fractions with unlike denominators (including mixed numbers) by replacing given fractions with equivalent fractions in such a way as to produce an equivalent sum or difference of fractions with like denominators.
2	D	Number & Operations-Fractions	Solve real-world problems involving division of unit fractions by non-zero whole numbers and division of whole numbers by unit fractions.
3	C	Number & Operations in Base Ten	Add, subtract, multiply, and divide decimals to hundredths.
4	A	Number & Operations in Base Ten	Add, subtract, multiply, and divide decimals to hundredths.
5	D	Number & Operations in Base Ten	Fluently multiply multi-digit whole numbers using the standard algorithm.
6	C	Number & Operations-Fractions	Interpret a fraction as division of the numerator by the denominator.
7	B	Geometry	Locate a point in a coordinate system by using an ordered pair of numbers, called its coordinates.
8	B	Number & Operations in Base Ten	Explain patterns in the placement of the decimal point when a decimal is multiplied or divided by a power of 10.
9	B	Number & Operations-Fractions	Add and subtract fractions with unlike denominators (including mixed numbers) by replacing given fractions with equivalent fractions in such a way as to produce an equivalent sum or difference of fractions with like denominators.
10	A	Number & Operations in Base Ten	Find whole-number quotients of whole numbers with up to four-digit dividends and two-digit divisors, using strategies based on place value, the properties of operations, and/or the relationship between multiplication and division.
11	C	Number & Operations in Base Ten	Add, subtract, multiply, and divide decimals to hundredths.
12	C	Geometry	Locate a point in a coordinate system by using an ordered pair of numbers, called its coordinates.
13	D	Number & Operations in Base Ten	Add, subtract, multiply, and divide decimals to hundredths.
14	D	Measurement & Data	Convert among different-sized standard measurement units within a given measurement system, and use these conversions in solving multi-step, real world problems.
15	D	Measurement & Data	Recognize volume as an attribute of solid figures and understand concepts of volume measurement.
16	C	Measurement & Data	Make a line plot to display a data set of measurements in fractions of a unit (1/2, 1/4, 1/8). Use operations on fractions for this grade to solve problems involving information presented in line plots.

17	A	Geometry	Use a coordinate system and understand that the first number indicates how far to travel from the origin in the direction of one axis, and the second number indicates how far to travel in the direction of the second axis.
18	C	Measurement & Data	Convert among different-sized standard measurement units within a given measurement system, and use these conversions in solving multi-step, real world problems.
19	D	Measurement & Data	Relate volume to the operations of multiplication and addition and solve real world and mathematical problems involving volume.
20	C	Number & Operations in Base Ten	Read and write decimals to thousandths using base-ten numerals, number names, and expanded form.
21	C	Measurement & Data	Convert among different-sized standard measurement units within a given measurement system, and use these conversions in solving multi-step, real world problems.
22	C	Measurement & Data	Convert among different-sized standard measurement units within a given measurement system, and use these conversions in solving multi-step, real world problems.
23	B	Measurement & Data	Measure volumes by counting unit cubes, using cubic cm, cubic in., cubic ft., and improvised units.
24	A	Operations/Algebraic Thinking	Generate two numerical patterns using two given rules. Identify apparent relationships between corresponding terms.
25	C	Operations/Algebraic Thinking	Form ordered pairs consisting of corresponding terms from the two patterns, and graph the ordered pairs on a coordinate plane.
26	D	Number & Operations in Base Ten	Find whole-number quotients of whole numbers with up to four-digit dividends and two-digit divisors, using strategies based on place value, the properties of operations, and/or the relationship between multiplication and division.
27	B	Number & Operations-Fractions	Add and subtract fractions with unlike denominators (including mixed numbers) by replacing given fractions with equivalent fractions in such a way as to produce an equivalent sum or difference of fractions with like denominators.
28	A	Number & Operations in Base Ten	Perform operations with multi-digit whole numbers.
29	C	Measurement & Data	Make a line plot to display a data set of measurements in fractions of a unit. Use operations on fractions for this grade to solve problems involving information presented in line plots.
30	D	Number & Operations-Fractions	Use benchmark fractions and number sense of fractions to estimate mentally and assess the reasonableness of answers.

Common Core Mathematics, Practice Set 6

Question	Answer	Topic	Next Generation Learning Standard
1	C	Measurement & Data	Relate volume to the operations of multiplication and addition and solve real world and mathematical problems involving volume.
2	B	Number & Operations in Base Ten	Perform operations with multi-digit whole numbers.
3	C	Geometry	Locate a point in a coordinate system by using an ordered pair of numbers, called its coordinates.
4	A	Geometry	Classify two-dimensional figures in a hierarchy based on properties.
5	B	Operations/Algebraic Thinking	Analyze patterns and relationships by identifying apparent relationships between corresponding terms.
6	C	Operations/Algebraic Thinking	Write simple expressions that record calculations with numbers, and interpret numerical expressions without evaluating them.
7	D	Measurement & Data	Convert among different-sized standard measurement units within a given measurement system, and use these conversions in solving multi-step, real world problems.
8	B	Operations/Algebraic Thinking	Apply the order of operations to evaluate numerical expressions.
9	D	Number & Operations in Base Ten	Use place value understanding to round decimals to any place.
10	B	Measurement & Data	Measure volumes by counting unit cubes, using cubic cm, cubic in., cubic ft., and improvised units.
11	B	Operations/Algebraic Thinking	Form ordered pairs consisting of corresponding terms from the two patterns, and graph the ordered pairs on a coordinate plane.
12	C	Operations/Algebraic Thinking	Write simple expressions that record calculations with numbers, and interpret numerical expressions without evaluating them.
13	B	Number & Operations in Base Ten	Read and write decimals to thousandths using base-ten numerals, number names, and expanded form.
14	B	Number & Operations in Base Ten	Explain patterns in the placement of the decimal point when a decimal is multiplied or divided by a power of 10.
15	D	Measurement & Data	Apply the formulas $V = l \times w \times h$ and $V = B \times h$ for rectangular prisms to find volumes of right rectangular prisms with whole-number edge lengths in the context of solving real world and mathematical problems.
16	C	Operations/Algebraic Thinking	Analyze patterns and relationships.
17	A	Number & Operations in Base Ten	Perform operations with multi-digit whole numbers.
18	C	Number & Operations-Fractions	Add and subtract fractions with unlike denominators (including mixed numbers) by replacing given fractions with equivalent fractions in such a way as to produce an equivalent sum or difference of fractions with like denominators.
19	C	Operations/Algebraic Thinking	Apply the order of operations to evaluate numerical expressions.

20	C	Number & Operations-Fractions	Solve word problems involving addition and subtraction of fractions referring to the same whole, including cases of unlike denominators.
21	A	Measurement & Data	Convert among different-sized standard measurement units within a given measurement system, and use these conversions in solving multi-step, real world problems.
22	B	Operations/Algebraic Thinking	Write simple expressions that record calculations with numbers, and interpret numerical expressions without evaluating them.
23	D	Operations/Algebraic Thinking	Write simple expressions that record calculations with numbers, and interpret numerical expressions without evaluating them.
24	B	Number & Operations-Fractions	Multiply fractional side lengths to find areas of rectangles, and represent fraction products as rectangular areas.
25	B	Geometry	Understand that attributes belonging to a category of two-dimensional figures also belong to all subcategories of that category.
26	D	Number & Operations in Base Ten	Fluently multiply multi-digit whole numbers using a standard algorithm.
27	B	Geometry	Classify two-dimensional figures in a hierarchy based on properties.
28	B	Number & Operations-Fractions	Explain why multiplying a given number by a fraction less than 1 results in a product smaller than the given number.
29	D	Measurement & Data	Convert among different-sized standard measurement units within a given measurement system when the conversion factor is given. Use these conversions in solving multi-step, real world problems.
30	C	Measurement & Data	Convert among different-sized standard measurement units within a given measurement system when the conversion factor is given.

Common Core Mathematics, Practice Set 7

Question	Points	Topic	Next Generation Learning Standard
1	3	Operations/Algebraic Thinking	Generate two numerical patterns using two given rules. Identify apparent relationships between corresponding terms. Form ordered pairs consisting of corresponding terms from the two patterns, and graph the ordered pairs on a coordinate plane.
2	3	Measurement & Data	Recognize volume as additive. Find volumes of solid figures composed of two non-overlapping right rectangular prisms by adding the volumes of the non-overlapping parts, applying this technique to solve real world problems.
3	3	Operations/Algebraic Thinking	Generate two numerical patterns using two given rules. Identify apparent relationships between corresponding terms.
4	3	Measurement & Data	Make a line plot to display a data set of measurements in fractions of a unit (1/2, 1/4, 1/8). Use operations on fractions for this grade to solve problems involving information presented in line plots.
5	2	Number & Operations in Base Ten	Find whole-number quotients of whole numbers with up to four-digit dividends and two-digit divisors, using strategies based on place value, the properties of operations, and/or the relationship between multiplication and division. Illustrate and explain the calculation by using equations, rectangular arrays, and/or area models.
6	2	Number & Operations in Base Ten	Add, subtract, multiply, and divide decimals to hundredths, using concrete models or drawings and strategies based on place value, properties of operations, and/or the relationship between addition and subtraction; relate the strategy to a written method and explain the reasoning used.
7	2	Measurement & Data	Measure volumes by counting unit cubes, using cubic cm, cubic in., cubic ft., and improvised units.
8	2	Geometry	Use a pair of perpendicular number lines, called axes, to define a coordinate system, with the intersection of the lines (the origin) arranged to coincide with the 0 on each line and a given point in the plane located by using an ordered pair of numbers, called its coordinates.
9	2	Operations/Algebraic Thinking	Apply the order of operations to evaluate numerical expressions.
10	2	Number & Operations-Fractions	Apply and extend previous understandings of multiplication to multiply a fraction or whole number by a fraction.

Q1.
The first table should be completed with the *y* values 0, 2, 4, and 6.
The second table should be completed with the *y* values 2, 4, 6, and 8.
The two lines should be graphed as shown below.

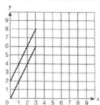

The student should give a reasonable comparison of the lines. The comparison should include that the lines are parallel and that the second line is 2 units above the first line.

Scoring Information
Give a total score out of 3.
Give a score of 1 for the tables correctly completed.
Give a score of 1 for the lines correctly graphed.
Give a score out of 1 for the comparison of the lines.

Q2.
The following two sets of dimensions should be listed. (Measurements can be listed in any order.)
10 cm by 2 cm by 2 cm and 4 cm by 8 cm by 2 cm
4 cm by 10 cm by 2 cm and 6 cm by 2 cm by 2 cm

Answer: 104 cubic centimeters or 104 cm³

Scoring Information
Give a total score out of 3.
Give a score of 1 for each set of correct dimensions.
Give a score of 1 for the correct answer.

Q3.
The student should complete the table with the following values:

Harris's Total Savings	3	6	9	12	15	18
Jamie's Total Savings	6	12	18	24	30	36

The student should explain that Jamie's total savings are always twice Harris's total savings.

Scoring Information
Give a total score out of 3.
Give a score of 1 for the correct values for Harris's Total Savings.
Give a score of 1 for the correct values for Jamie's Total Savings.
Give a score out of 1 for the explanation.

Q4.
The work should show the completed graph as below.

Hailstone Diameter (inches)

```
        X
        X               X       X
        X       X       X       X       X       X
 ───────────────────────────────────────────────────────
  0     1       1       3       1       5       3       7       1
        ─       ─       ─       ─       ─       ─       ─
        8       4       8       2       8       4       8
```

Answer: $\frac{5}{8}$ inches

Scoring Information
Give a total score out of 3.
Give a score out of 2 for the line plot.
Give a score of 1 for the correct answer.

Q5.
Equation: $448 = 32h$
Answer: $14

Scoring Information
Give a total score out of 2.
Give a score of 1 for the correct equation.
Give a score of 1 for the correct answer.

Q6.
0.8 miles

The work may show calculating 2.6 − 1.8. The work may also shade the diagram to find the difference.

Scoring Information
Give a total score out of 2.
Give a score of 1 for the correct answer.
Give a score out of 1 for the working.

Q7.
60 cubic centimeters

The work may show the calculation 3 × 4 × 5 = 60. The work may also show counting 3 rows of 20 or 5 columns of 12.

Scoring Information
Give a total score out of 2.
Give a score of 1 for the correct answer.
Give a score out of 1 for the working.

Q8.
(2, 4)
(9, 9)

Scoring Information
Give a total score out of 2.
Give a score of 1 for each correct answer.

Q9.
Expression: $(4 \times 3) + (7 \times 5)$
Answer: $47

Scoring Information
Give a total score out of 2.
Give a score of 1 for the correct expression.
Give a score of 1 for the correct answer.

Q10.
80

The work may show the calculation of $200 \times \frac{2}{5}$. The work could also divide 200 by 5 to find one-fifth and then multiply the result by 2.

Scoring Information
Give a total score out of 2.
Give a score of 1 for the correct answer.
Give a score out of 1 for the working.

Common Core Mathematics, Practice Set 8

Question	Answer	Topic	Next Generation Learning Standard
1	B	Number & Operations in Base Ten	Add, subtract, multiply, and divide decimals to hundredths, using concrete models or drawings.
2	A	Number & Operations-Fractions	Add and subtract fractions with unlike denominators (including mixed numbers).
3	D	Number & Operations-Fractions	Interpret division of a whole number by a unit fraction, and compute such quotients.
4	B	Geometry	Classify two-dimensional figures in a hierarchy based on properties.
5	B	Number & Operations in Base Ten	Fluently multiply multi-digit whole numbers using a standard algorithm.
6	C	Number & Operations-Fractions	Interpret division of a unit fraction by a non-zero whole number, and compute such quotients.
7	D	Operations/Algebraic Thinking	Apply the order of operations to evaluate numerical expressions.
8	B	Measurement & Data	Convert among different-sized standard measurement units within a given measurement system, and use these conversions in solving multi-step, real world problems.
9	C	Number & Operations-Fractions	Interpret a fraction as division of the numerator by the denominator.
10	D	Number & Operations-Fractions	Solve word problems involving addition and subtraction of fractions referring to the same whole, including cases of unlike denominators.
11	D	Number & Operations in Base Ten	Fluently multiply multi-digit whole numbers using a standard algorithm.
12	C	Number & Operations-Fractions	Interpret a fraction as division of the numerator by the denominator.
13	B	Measurement & Data	Convert among different-sized standard measurement units within a given measurement system, and use these conversions in solving multi-step, real world problems.
14	C	Operations/Algebraic Thinking	Analyze patterns and relationships by identifying apparent relationships between corresponding terms.
15	D	Number & Operations in Base Ten	Find whole-number quotients of whole numbers with up to four-digit dividends and two-digit divisors, using strategies based on properties of operations.
16	A	Geometry	Classify two-dimensional figures in a hierarchy based on properties.
17	D	Geometry	Locate a point in a coordinate system by using an ordered pair of numbers, called its coordinates.
18	B	Operations/Algebraic Thinking	Analyze patterns and relationships by identifying apparent relationships between corresponding terms.
19	C	Measurement & Data	Recognize volume as an attribute of solid figures and understand concepts of volume measurement.
20	D	Geometry	Classify two-dimensional figures in a hierarchy based on properties.
21	B	Operations/Algebraic Thinking	Write simple expressions that record calculations with numbers, and interpret numerical expressions without evaluating them.

22	B	Geometry	Use a coordinate system and understand that the first number indicates how far to travel from the origin in the direction of one axis, and the second number indicates how far to travel in the direction of the second axis.
23	B	Number & Operations in Base Ten	Explain patterns in the placement of the decimal point when a decimal is multiplied or divided by a power of 10.
24	D	Number & Operations in Base Ten	Read and write decimals to thousandths using base-ten numerals, number names, and expanded form.
25	C	Operations/Algebraic Thinking	Apply the order of operations to evaluate numerical expressions.
26	B	Operations/Algebraic Thinking	Write simple expressions that record calculations with numbers, and interpret numerical expressions without evaluating them.
27	D	Measurement & Data	Find the volume of a right rectangular prism with whole-number side lengths by packing it with unit cubes, and show that the volume is the same as would be found by multiplying the edge lengths, equivalently by multiplying the height by the area of the base.
28	D	Number & Operations-Fractions	Solve real-world problems involving division of unit fractions by non-zero whole numbers and division of whole numbers by unit fractions.
29	A	Number & Operations-Fractions	Interpret a fraction as division of the numerator by the denominator.
30	D	Number & Operations-Fractions	Apply and extend previous understandings of multiplication to multiply a fraction or whole number by a fraction.

Common Core Mathematics, Practice Set 9

Question	Answer	Topic	Next Generation Learning Standard
1	A	Geometry	Classify two-dimensional figures in a hierarchy based on properties.
2	D	Operations/Algebraic Thinking	Analyze patterns and relationships by identifying apparent relationships between corresponding terms.
3	D	Operations/Algebraic Thinking	Write simple expressions that record calculations with numbers, and interpret numerical expressions without evaluating them.
4	A	Number & Operations in Base Ten	Use place value understanding to round decimals to any place.
5	C	Operations/Algebraic Thinking	Apply the order of operations to evaluate numerical expressions.
6	B	Operations/Algebraic Thinking	Analyze patterns and relationships by identifying apparent relationships between corresponding terms.
7	A	Number & Operations in Base Ten	Find whole-number quotients of whole numbers with up to four-digit dividends and two-digit divisors, using strategies based on place value, the properties of operations, and/or the relationship between multiplication and division.
8	D	Number & Operations in Base Ten	Compare two decimals to thousandths based on meanings of the digits in each place, using >, =, and < symbols to record the results of comparisons.
9	A	Number & Operations-Fractions	Interpret a fraction as division of the numerator by the denominator. Solve word problems involving division of whole numbers leading to answers in the form of fractions or mixed numbers.
10	C	Operations/Algebraic Thinking	Analyze patterns and relationships by identifying apparent relationships between corresponding terms.
11	B	Number & Operations in Base Ten	Compare two decimals to thousandths based on meanings of the digits in each place, using >, =, and < symbols to record the results of comparisons.
12	A	Number & Operations in Base Ten	Find whole-number quotients of whole numbers with up to four-digit dividends and two-digit divisors, using strategies based on the relationship between multiplication and division.
13	A	Number & Operations in Base Ten	Illustrate and explain calculations by using equations, rectangular arrays, and/or area models.
14	D	Number & Operations in Base Ten	Explain patterns in the placement of the decimal point when a decimal is multiplied or divided by a power of 10.
15	D	Geometry	Understand that attributes belonging to a category of two-dimensional figures also belong to all subcategories of that category.
16	A	Number & Operations-Fractions	Explain why multiplying a given number by a fraction greater than 1 results in a product greater than the given number.
17	C	Operations/Algebraic Thinking	Generate two numerical patterns using two given rules. Identify apparent relationships between corresponding terms.
18	D	Number & Operations in Base Ten	Perform operations with multi-digit whole numbers.
19	B	Number & Operations in Base Ten	Perform operations with multi-digit whole numbers.

20	D	Number & Operations in Base Ten	Find whole-number quotients of whole numbers. Illustrate and explain the calculation by using equations, rectangular arrays, and/or area models.
21	D	Operations/Algebraic Thinking	Write simple expressions that record calculations with numbers, and interpret numerical expressions without evaluating them.
22	B	Operations/Algebraic Thinking	Analyze patterns and relationships by identifying apparent relationships between corresponding terms.
23	A	Geometry	Classify two-dimensional figures in a hierarchy based on properties.
24	B	Number & Operations in Base Ten	Recognize that in a multi-digit number, a digit in one place represents 10 times as much as it represents in the place to its right and 1/10 of what it represents in the place to its left.
25	C	Number & Operations-Fractions	Interpret multiplication as scaling (resizing) by comparing the size of a product to the size of one factor on the basis of the size of the other factor, without performing the indicated multiplication.
26	A	Geometry	Classify two-dimensional figures in a hierarchy based on properties.
27	D	Measurement & Data	Convert among different-sized standard measurement units within a given measurement system when the conversion factor is given. Use these conversions in solving multi-step, real world problems.
28	A	Measurement & Data	Recognize volume as additive. Find volumes of solid figures composed of two non-overlapping right rectangular prisms by adding the volumes of the non-overlapping parts, applying this technique to solve real world problems.
29	D	Number & Operations-Fractions	Solve real-world problems involving division of unit fractions by non-zero whole numbers and division of whole numbers by unit fractions.
30	D	Geometry	Represent real world and mathematical problems by graphing points in the first quadrant of the coordinate plane, and interpret coordinate values of points in the context of the situation.

Common Core Mathematics, Practice Set 10

Question	Points	Topic	Next Generation Learning Standard
1	3	Measurement & Data	Find the volume of a right rectangular prism with whole-number side lengths by packing it with unit cubes, and show that the volume is the same as would be found by multiplying the edge lengths, equivalently by multiplying the height by the area of the base.
2	2	Geometry	Represent real world and mathematical problems by graphing points in the first quadrant of the coordinate plane.
3	2	Geometry	Represent real world and mathematical problems by graphing points in the first quadrant of the coordinate plane, and interpret coordinate values of points in the context of the situation.
4	3	Geometry	Understand that attributes belonging to a category of two-dimensional figures also belong to all subcategories of that category.
5	2	Geometry	Classify two-dimensional figures in a hierarchy based on properties.
6	3	Number & Operations-Fractions	Solve word problems involving addition and subtraction of fractions referring to the same whole, including cases of unlike denominators. Apply and extend previous understandings of multiplication to multiply a fraction or whole number by a fraction.
7	2	Number & Operations in Base Ten	Add, subtract, multiply, and divide decimals to hundredths, using strategies based on place value and properties of operations.
8	2	Number & Operations in Base Ten	Use place value understanding to round decimals to any place.
9	2	Measurement & Data	Convert among different-sized standard measurement units within a given measurement system, and use these conversions in solving multi-step, real world problems.
10	3	Measurement & Data	Relate volume to the operations of multiplication and addition and solve real world and mathematical problems involving volume.

Q1.
16 inches

Each column in the table should be completed with any combination of length, height, and width that multiply to 64. Possible answers include: 4, 8, and 2; 64, 1, and 1; 8, 8, and 1; or 32, 2, and 1.

The student should identify that Bradley could make a cube. The explanation should describe how the cube would have side lengths of 4 and a volume of 64 cubic inches. The explanation may include the calculation 4 × 4 × 4 = 64.

Scoring Information
Give a total score out of 3.
Give a score of 1 for a correct answer of 16 inches.
Give a score of 1 for the table completed correctly.
Give a score out of 1 for identifying that Bradley could make a cube and providing an explanation.

Q2.
The table should be completed with the *y* values 1, 4, 7, and 10.
The line should be graphed as shown below.

Scoring Information
Give a total score out of 2.
Give a score of 1 for completing the table correctly.
Give a score of 1 for the line correctly graphed.

Q3.
(8, 8)

The student may describe the calculation (6 + 2, 5 + 3) = (8, 8), or may describe plotting the new point on the grid and reading the coordinates.

Scoring Information
Give a total score out of 2.
Give a score of 1 for the correct answer.
Give a score out of 1 for the explanation.

Q4.
BA and CD, BC and AD

The student should identify that the shape is a rhombus. The explanation should refer to the two pairs of parallel sides and the four sides being equal in length. The explanation may also include that the shape is not a square because the angles are not right angles.

Scoring Information
Give a total score out of 3.
Give a score of 0.5 for each correct pair listed.
Give a score of 1 for the correct shape identified.
Give a score out of 1 for the explanation.

Q5.
The student should circle the statement below.
At least 1 pair of parallel sides

The student should identify that 4 congruent sides could be used to tell the difference between a rectangle and a square. The answer should show an understanding that all the statements are true for both rectangles and squares except that a square has 4 congruent sides and a rectangle does not.

Scoring Information
Give a total score out of 2.
Give a score of 1 for the correct statement circled.
Give a score out of 1 for identifying the correct statement and providing an explanation.

Q6.
Part A

$$\frac{7}{24}$$

The student may add the three fractions to find $\frac{17}{24}$ and then calculate $1 - \frac{17}{24} = \frac{7}{24}$.

The student may convert all the fractions to those with denominators of 24, and then calculate $\frac{24}{24} - \frac{6}{24} - \frac{9}{24} - \frac{2}{24} = \frac{7}{24}$.

The student could also use a diagram to find the remaining fraction, such as the one below.

Pumpkin	Pumpkin	Pumpkin	Apple	Apple	Apple
Pumpkin	Pumpkin	Pumpkin	Apple	Apple	Apple
Pumpkin	Pumpkin	Pumpkin	Peach	Peach	Peach
Cherry	Cherry	Peach	Peach	Peach	Peach

Part B
30

The work should show the calculation of $360 \times \frac{1}{12} = 30$. The work could show an understanding that $360 \times \frac{1}{12}$ is the same as $\frac{360}{12}$ or $360 \div 12$.

Scoring Information
Give a total score out of 3.
Give a score of 1 for the correct answer to Part A.
Give a score of 1 for the correct answer to Part B.
Give a score out of 1 for the working.

Q7.
$27.80

The work could show the sum of all the decimals in one step. The work could also show adding the two sets of decimals that give whole numbers, and then adding the final decimal, as shown below.
$(5.73 + 5.27) + (5.49 + 5.51) + 5.80 \rightarrow 11 + 11 + 5.80 = 27.80$

Scoring Information
Give a total score out of 2.
Give a score of 1 for the correct answer.
Give a score out of 1 for the working.

Q8.
The number 3.8 should be plotted on the number line.
Answer: 4

Scoring Information
Give a total score out of 2.
Give a score of 1 for the number correctly plotted.
Give a score of 1 for the correct answer.

Q9.
The measurements 6000 mm and 6 m should be circled.
0.006 kilometers

Scoring Information
Give a total score out of 2.
Give a score of 0.5 for each correct measurement circled.
Give a score of 1 for the correct answer.

Q10.
The student should write and solve the equation 2 × 2 × 4 = 16.
Volume: 16 cubic centimeters

The student should identify that the volume would double if the height doubled. The student could explain that doubling one of the values in the calculation doubles the result. The student could also double the height and show that 4 × 2 × 4 = 32, which is double 16.

Scoring Information
Give a total score out of 3.
Give a score of 1 for a correct equation.
Give a score of 1 for the correct volume.
Give a score out of 1 for the explanation.

Get to Know Our Product Range

Mathematics

Practice Workbooks
Practice sets and practice tests will prepare students for the state tests.

Common Core Quiz Books
Focused individual quizzes cover every math skill one by one.

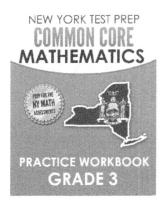 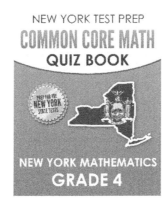 

Reading

Practice Workbooks
Practice sets and practice tests will prepare students for the state tests.

Reading Skills Workbooks
Short passages and question sets will develop and improve reading comprehension skills and are perfect for ongoing test prep.

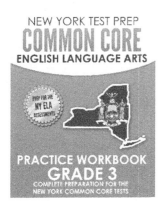 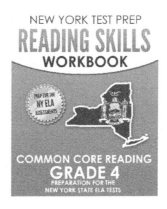 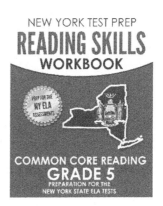

Writing

Writing Skills Workbooks
Students write narratives, essays, and arguments, and write in response to passages.

Narrative and Argument Writing Workbooks
Guided workbooks teach all the skills needed to write narratives and arguments.

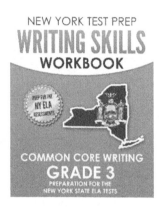 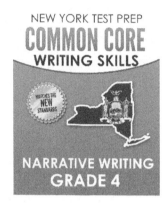 

Language and Vocabulary

Language and Vocabulary Quiz Books
Focused quizzes cover spelling, grammar, usage, writing conventions, and vocabulary.

Revising and Editing Workbooks
Students improve language skills and writing skills by identifying and correcting errors.

Language Skills Workbooks
Exercises on specific language skills including figurative language, synonyms, and homographs.

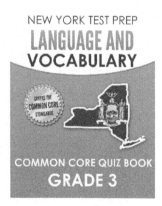 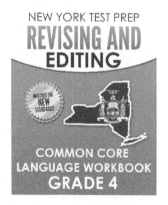 

http://www.testmasterpress.com

Made in the
USA
Middletown, DE